BATTLE CRY

A Call to Arms Against Human Trafficking

Amanda Foltz

Battle Cry

A Call to Arms Against Human Trafficking

Author: Amanda Foltz

Editor: Jesse Dunlap

Scripture references from New King James Version of the Bible.

Copyright ©1985 by Thomas Nelson Publishers

For further information email:

hello@amandafoltz.com

DEDICATION

To God, my Savior, Jesus Christ,
who rescued me from a life of hurt and pain

To the best family a girl could ask for:
Joshua, Cody, Zion, and Hero

To all my Followers and Supporters

ACKNOWLEDGMENTS

Without these amazing people in my life I would not be able to GO into the world and create change:
I give all the glory to God, my Savior, Jesus Christ, who rescued me from a life of hurt and pain, who graciously allows me to be part of restoring others.

My incredibly patient husband, Joshua:
Thank you for your unyielding support, allowing me to go to dangerous countries so that I can spread God's love.

The best kids a girl could ask for:Cody, Zion, and Hero
Thank you for allowing me to travel, drag you to meetings, and patiently wait for me as I talk to strangers in coffee shop lines about human trafficking.

My editor - Jesse Dunlap. Thank you for all the time and effort you put into making sure all the random thoughts and ideas in my head made it on paper in a clear way

All my friends and readers:
Thank you for following, sharing, and supporting me and my journey.

I truly hope that you learn and grow from this book. My desire is for you to take this information and expand upon it. That you will GO and be the change this world needs, and that you will GO in love and spread your light around the whole world.

CONTENTS

FOREWORD
By Kelly Dore

Human Trafficking is nearly a $150 Billion Dollar a year business around the world. There are no political, socioeconomic, cultural or ethnic boundaries that protect one population of vulnerable people from another. Human Trafficking consists of Labor and Sex Trafficking, with many facets and variations outlined by United Nations and Countries who are committed to ending Modern Day Slavery. The one constant factor contributing to Human Trafficking is MAN. Since the beginning of time, wherever people coexist with each other, there has been someone exerting force, coercion or control over them willing to use another human being for product, profit or pleasure. It is a moral conundrum that transcends across all continents, countries and state lines. Human Trafficking is not just a developing world problem, it is very real in every first world country as well. In the US, it is estimated that nearly 83% of sex trafficking victims are US citizens and nearly 50% are minors- under the age of 18, boys and girls.

Many times, it is something that communities need to be educated on, while Human Trafficking has made headlines across the country in various new forms, it is not something that many people understand or acknowledge is happening within their own communities. How can we address a problem if we do not know it exists and better yet, how can we solve a problem if we cannot see it entirely in front of us? This is what many non-profit organizations, government agencies and survivor leaders across the country are trying to answer, yet there has not been a solid agreement on how to best collaborate or how to best get people involved with this issue. Battle Cry gives a basic narrative on what the issue of Human Sex Trafficking in America looks like, what people need to know about it, how to respond to it and most importantly, how to act. Every problem needs a solution, yet many people do not know where to start. This book will help the reader figure out their passion, how to engage and how to become an advocate for someone without a voice.

Often, human beings do not directly mean to ignore a social problem, especially if there is a human rights violation, however, they do not respond because they do not see what is sometimes directly in front of them. Battle Cry gives the reader a good base to understand and see the problem right here in America. When we think of human trafficking, child slavery or sexual servitude, we often think of children being kidnapped, the sensationalized media images of children in chains, bound or gagged, and we think of them being immigrant children, smuggled into this country who largely remain unseen. The fact is that most children in America who are sex trafficking victims, are in fact, US born citizens, who have found themselves in a situation, due to their social and societal circumstance. The largest majority of children who are sexually trafficked in the US are children in the foster care system, children who have unstable family lives and who run from those settings. Due to abuse, neglect or addiction issues with the adults charged to care for and protect them, there are many reasons why children become vulnerable in society and end up being victims of human trafficking. There is also a percentage of children who are trafficking by their own families, people who are familiar to them or their family, or people they meet online and become acquaintances with. Poverty and lack of education have widely become the most prevalent reasons for the vulnerability that exists with human trafficking victims, because when there are no options for someone to create a better life for themselves, there is no choice but to survive the only way they know how. In many cases, the sexual abuse began at a young age for the victim and there is no concept of self-worth or dignity, because this was normalized so early on.

My organization always gets the same questions, 1). What can be done to better educate my friends and neighbors on this horrific form of slavery and 2). What are some ways to get involved, I want to help, but I do not know what to do?

Amanda Foltz has extensive knowledge and first-hand experience in to the world of sexual servitude and Battle Cry will not only define what this problem looks like in the US, but how to understand the impacts of our own social existence, whether it be through consumerism or working with organizations and how to answer the call. Her step by step guide is one way for everyday people to get involved with this epidemic. Amanda has interviewed and worked with survivors of sex trafficking to understand how to best represent and help them heal from their experiences. We must recognize that not every organization who says they are helping victims does and not every organization is financially prudent and transparent about what they are doing. There are many organizations who are formed to support survivors, yet, only a small handful are on the ground doing the work. Battle Cry gives good insight to this and for the volunteer to best choose which organization is ethical, trauma-informed, and sustainable for the long-term recovery of survivors of human sex trafficking.

As with anything, you personally get invested into, whether it be through time or treasure, Battle Cry will lay out how you can volunteer, how you can make an impact in the area that you are most comfortable. Not everyone can be on the front lines, there needs to be people every step of the way to support the call to action and everyone of those positions is valuable to the cause. We must remember that when we are working with human beings, God has given us all the civil, fundamental and natural inalienable rights to be free and have free will. We can "rescue" shelter animals and give them a home, but we cannot "rescue" human beings. Human beings have free will to choose their freedom and they have the responsibility for taking ownership of that freedom. It is not an easy task, and this is the fundamental issue for victims, johns and pimps, how are we the best stewards of our own free will? These separate people ethically and morally from each other, yet, we all must coexist on the same planet and work towards the betterment of humanity. Amanda's book is a great look into important conversations that we must have with ourselves and each other about who we choose to be. It is an honor to work beside Amanda in her call to arms against human trafficking. For survivors of human sex trafficking, this is our Battle Cry, please join us and help us continue to fight for the most vulnerable in society.

—Kelly Dore

Executive Director of
National Human Trafficking
Survivor Coalition

WHENEVER I HEAR ANYONE ARGUING FOR
SLAVERY, I FEEL A STRONG IMPULSE TO SEE
IT TRIED ON HIM PERSONALLY
-ABRAHAM LINCOLN

INTRODUCTION

INTRODUCTION

Take a moment to imagine yourself in modern-day America on a beautiful, clear day. Lawn mowers are buzzing up and down yards, moms are pushing strollers down immaculately maintained walkways, and the neighborhood school is filled with the laughter of kids at recess.

Walk with me and let's visit the house on the corner. It's possible you live near one just like it, where cars randomly pull in and out of the driveway. You believe you know who lives there, but you can't place their face—only occasionally do you catch a glimpse of them pulling into their garage. Is it the obscurity of their life that makes you wonder who they really are. Or is it the feeling in your gut telling you not to trust that house or those inside it? Everything on the outside looks normal, cared for, and they seem nice enough. So, why can't you shake that feeling? Let's go inside this normal, well-kept home and see what we find.

Standing on the front porch, you notice there are cameras everywhere and a heavy security system. That's odd, you think. As you go inside, you walk through the finely decorated living room, past the kitchen with granite counter tops, and open the basement door. Something in your stomach turns. Your gut is starting to talk to you. Something is not right here. On the outside it looks like an average track home with manicured lawns and a white picket fence. So, why do you have a feeling there is a darkness lingering here?

You open the basement door and start to walk down the stairs. It's dim and as your eyes adjust, you try to register what you are seeing. There are mattresses lining the unpainted cement walls. Is that a young girl in a racy red dress sitting on a mattress? She couldn't be older than thirteen. The makeup painted on her, the outfit she wears, and the stained mattress, all tell a story you don't want to believe.

What is really happening in this home?

That's a great question with a disheartening answer. It's what this book is all about: To bring the things that are happening in the dark, into the light. To make you aware of what is going on in basements and backrooms all around you.

This little girl inside the perfect suburban home is a sex slave. Men pay money to receive sexual favors from her. Intercourse, blowjobs, anal sex, or worse. If she does not perform, she will be beaten, her vagina burned with cigarettes, and her family threatened. She must deliver sex on demand, or else. This child is sitting here with makeup piled on her delicate young face to hide the bruises covering her. Shaking and scared, just waiting for her next John to arrive and fulfill his sexual fantasies using her little body. When he leaves, he will be temporary fulfilled but she will be left broken.

Now that your eyes are adjusting, you realize there is more than just one girl here, all of them too young to have their innocence ripped away. You are not the first person descending these stairs today and you won't be the last.

Questions must be flooding your mind right now as you're putting the pieces together.

Questions like: How can an operation survive in a neighborhood like this? Where did these girls come from? Who is paying for sex with young girls?

This book is to inform you and encourage you to dig deeper into the truth. This book will answer some tough questions and, in the end, leave you with firm answers on how you can make a difference in these young girls' lives.

To answer the question-
Who is paying to have sex with these young girls?

Simple answer: It's the dad cheering for his kid at the soccer game. The family doctor. The businessman. The person you would never expect. That's why the traffickers have her here in the suburbs: It's where their clientele lives, works, and hides.

You just witnessed child sex slavery. This type of slavery falls under the definition of "human trafficking." There are many ways to observe human trafficking, and many different places, shapes and forms it takes. I feel, too many people are surprised to find out that this crime is thriving in America. It's in the big and small cities, downtowns, and yes— the suburbs. It's all around us.

This subject is not an easy one to read about for the first time. This is a book on human trafficking, and you picked it up for a reason. It's possible you've heard the term "human trafficking" and are curious what it means. Maybe, you heard stories of little girls being sold for sex and wanted to go rescue them. It's also plausible that a friend told you about this book and insisted you read it. Or, perhaps my well-branded cover caught your eye. Whatever the reason for you holding this book now, I believe it was meant to be.

What you are about to read and discover will forever change you. It forever changed me. You will cry, scream, yell and possibly get sick to your stomach.

I've got you, friend. I've been there.

If you read this book and never think about its subject again, I don't blame you. When I first joined this war, it was brutal. I would tell others about human trafficking everywhere I went, there were two primary ways my audience would react— after turning various shades of white, red, or green.

The first reaction was to ignore it completely. Forget or pretend you didn't just hear about this and go about your life. If that is you, no judgments here. This fight is not for everyone. There are plenty of great organizations that need help. I have many friends fighting for many different causes around the world. Like no-kill shelters or clean water in Africa. I've been to Africa and they absolutely need clean water. There is much to help within this world, and there is no lack of amazing causes to join. I encourage you to keep reading and complete the personality and strength finder in the back of this book. It can help bring clarity to anyone with any type of cause.

But if you are anything like me, yours will be the second response. You will hear about this and be unable to sleep for days. You will want to throw up, and then throw down. You will want to get on the next plane, punch someone in the face, and rescue as many children as you can. You are enraged. You are terrified. You never want to let your kids out of the house again! You want to do something to stop this.

No, you must do something to stop this. If this is you, then buy the book, read it, pass it out and join us in the battle against human trafficking.

This book is a practical application for what anyone can do in their free time to join the fight against human trafficking. It's the small things we do with great love that make a difference and set the captives free. Let's face it, if you are reading this book, you are not average. You are an extraordinary individual who cares.

This book is also meant to equip organizations to collaborate with volunteers and empower them. Non-profits are struggling to make progress and keep volunteers engaged. By understanding an individuals strengths and passion we can better equip them to join the fight.

Let this book be a guide to how individuals, volunteers, and organizations can all join forces and start making a lasting impact as we fight to end human trafficking.

Will you answer the call to arms and join in the battle cry?

NOTES

THE REAL WORK OF OUR LIVES IS TO
BECOME AWARE + AWAKENED. TO ANSWER
THE CALL
-OPRAH WINFREY

1 CHAPTER ONE
A Reason to Fight

1

Some people have the most fantastic way of telling a story. Before you know it, you find yourself holding your breath, and every sentence takes you deeper into the characters' world. It is an incredible gift to be able to help someone experience another world and truly feel part of it.

We are all connected through each other's stories and testimonies. As we listen and understand what others have overcome, it allows us to become sensitive to those around us and empowers us to change. We gain wisdom as to why others behave the way they do and where their passion is powered from. Testimonies of triumph empower people to overcome their own struggles. When we know what someone else has been through we can share in their experience, it creates an unbreakable bond. Stories unite the world. Love conquers all.

We all have a story within us. We've all gone through a battle that has forged us into the person we are today. Each of our stories is different, and yet, still the same. Our stories make us who we are today. Some of us keep our stories deep down inside, hoping no one will ever discover them. Some of us tell everyone and anyone who will listen. Others cannot tell their story because they have been silenced, they are in bondage, or no longer with us. It's for those who cannot speak for themselves that I tell you this story today.

It was a typical day around the Foltz house. Toys were thrown everywhere, kids ran wild, and I was frantically trying to clean up before the next client came over for a haircut. This was back in 2008 and my children were still toddlers. They were at those perfect ages where you could still manage to keep them in line but they weren't too cool for hugs from mom. My oldest son was barely ten years old, my middle son was seven and the youngest son was barely two. Yep, a mom of three boys!

My husband was going to college and finishing up his last year of school while maintaining a full-time job. I had just taken the leap to go from a full-time W2 employee to a full-time entrepreneur and opened a salon in my house. The kids were in a charter school across the city; the carpool seemed to be all encompassing on my day. Each day I would shuttle them to and from school, leaving a small window to fit in clients at my hair salon.

Time or money wasn't something any of us had in excess, to say the least. Most of my prayers back then were about needing more time, money—and most of all—sanity. We were living in a small city called Colorado Springs, Colorado at the time (about a 1.5-hour drive to Denver).

One day, my friend called me up and said I should come to see this movie with her; it was only showing in Denver and was one night only. She said that because of my past, no matter what, I need to make it to this movie. She was very insistent. I didn't understand what the movie was about, but her urgency piqued my interest. She was one of the few people who knew about my past life.

My past life. Now, that could fill a whole book of its own. It was full of sexual abuse and drugs. I would escape one bad situation only to be drawn into another. Rape started to become my new normal. I started to expect men to treat me that way and believed that was all I was worth. Every time we moved, I would pray things would be different and that I would find happiness, but I would only find pain. After a series of sexually abusive events when I was in the Air Force and then a suicide attempt, I found myself plunged even deeper into the darkness. I lost the fight within me and gave into the value I felt

3

the world had placed on me. I started to strip at a bikini club. The smoke, darkness, and men harassing me was where I felt the universe wanted me. I knew this world of pain. It was familiar to me. I knew what to expect from the men and from those who used me. The drugs kept me numb. I waited for death to find me. I would dream about being found dead in a gutter. I would envision people standing over my dead body shaking their heads and just walk by. I believed my purpose in life was to be used. I lost my fight. I was lost and had succumbed to the will others had for my life.

I escaped the sex industry when I found out I was pregnant with my first son. It was at a Planned Parenthood clinic when I heard the words, "you are pregnant." They wanted me to get an abortion right away because I was five months along. I walked out of that place stunned. I knew I didn't want an abortion, and now I had found a reason to fight for, this tiny life inside of me must live. My miracle began to unfold as I chose life and ran towards freedom. I threw a prayer up into the air, hoping that God would care about this life inside of me.

This innocent life inside of me had not done anything wrong. So, I prayed, "God, please make this baby okay. I will serve you all the days of my life. I promise I will be good and do good things. Please, God, don't let harm come to this little life inside of me."

That was the prayer that changed my life. I found the courage to run away and seek help. I moved from Florida to Colorado and moved back in with my mom. I even started to attend church. I thought for sure they would kick me out. All I owned was stripper heels and I didn't look or dress like the other girls. But I managed to find a church that let me in.

After a few months my mom told me I had to move out due to the advice her psychologist gave her. This left me homeless with a little baby, still trying to learn how to "fit in." I was learning how to speak and act appropriately, how to be a mom, a Christian, and how to not allow others to tell me my worth. I was learning how to live in freedom, how to love again, how to accept love. I met my husband at the college youth group, and we were married shortly after. I was rescued, redeemed, a mother and a wife. All I knew was that God rescued me, and I just wanted to do something to return the favor. There is a Bible verse about those forgiven much love much. This became my life verse.

So many people around me could not comprehend the life I escaped. My friend who invited me to the movie was one of the very few who accepted me and loved me freely. If she thought that I should go because of my past, I had to see this movie. I'm so happy I didn't use money or time as an excuse not to go. My husband, Joshua, and I made the drive to Denver and went to go see Call + Response.

The movie was playing at this chic-little theater off of Broadway Street. I remember thinking how cute the theater was. It had that old, timeless musty smell to it, red velvet covered everything and when you walked in, for a moment you could forget you're a mom of three boys and feel trendy and hip again. If I only I was prepared for what came next.

The lights dimmed, and the smell of popcorn filled the room. That was the last time I would be without a deep purpose in my life.

The movie started, and my heart dropped. What in the world was I watching? There was no way this could be real, I thought. I watched as movie stars and musicians used their platforms to tell stories for those who could not. Little girls being sold for sex. Children being sold for less than cattle. Story after story of people in bondage as slaves. Little girls being forced to give blow jobs, anal sex, and service men all day long. The movie quoted there were 2.7 million slaves in this world.

That number stuck with me. I watched those little girls on that screen, and tears flooded my face along with streaks of mascara and broken pieces of my heart. I could barely breathe.

My personal story felt so far from what these girls were going through. I know all too well—like many of you—the horrors of sexual violence, rape and mistreatment. I knew the pain and scars that my past created, and I couldn't imagine living the lives of these little girls. Being trapped in glass boxes and sold over and over again. I escaped my nightmare and I had to help them. But how? I was now a mom with three boys, a wife, and a business owner. I was barely making it, emotionally, mentally and financially. How could I ever help them?

The Bible verse in proverbs about speaking up for those who cannot speak for themselves lodged itself in my heart forever that day. I wanted to do what those musicians and actors were doing in the documentary. They were using their talents to speak for those little girls trapped in sex slavery. And so, my journey began.

My journey to answer the call to arms against human trafficking didn't begin with me starting a non-profit, traveling the world and winning a Noble Peace Prize—although at times I would feel like a failure because I had not accomplished such things. It took me a while to understand the truth behind being the change. It's not the awards, praises, or acknowledgements you receive that matters. It's how much you loved and reached out to help others that makes the greatest difference. It's doing small things with great love.

I was a work-from-home mom raising three boys who at times had different plans for my life than I did. They were not the easiest-going boys to parent; I guess boys never are. My family always came first, and that's the way I wanted it. Many times, I would have to step back from my volunteer work to focus on getting them through the next burst of hormones and growing pains. My desire in writing this book is to make sure you never feel like I did. No matter how you view your contribution to ending human trafficking, you need to realize that it's the small things that matter most.

Every little thing that I did was making an impact. I just may not have seen it that day, month or year. It's like those mosaic photos where you look at one picture from far away, but when you get up close, it's a thousand little photos. That's you and me.

Together, the small gestures we do to fight human trafficking make a significant impact.

We will become the butterfly effect. It's my favorite example of change. You see, one small, beautiful thing can cause a life-changing event. Just by being its beautiful self, a butterfly can change the world. though it may never know the impact it's made. The Chaos theory is a beautiful belief. It states that you cannot move one speck of sand without affecting the whole beach. A simple flutter from the wings of a butterfly can cause a tsunami weeks later.

As you read this book, note the things that stand out to you. Consider what you can do with what you have and where you are planted. The following chapters will go over what human trafficking is, the different forms it takes, and ideas on how you can make an impact.

Here I was, a mother of three boys, living barely above the poverty line, married with a husband who has a drive to succeed, and me—a mom who wanted to help others, raise her children and support her husband. And so, it was in that same year, my husband graduated and found new employment. This new job meant we no longer had to stand in welfare lines, it was the fresh start we were looking for financially. We also helped launch a new church, and since the church and job were in

Denver, we moved to the big city to start a new life. The very same city that turned my heart and created in me a passion for seeing the captives set free.

During this time, I started to devour books, articles, movies, and just about everything else I could find on human trafficking. Tears would flood my face as I read story after story about little children being beaten, drugged and abused. Stories about how it was so easy for anyone to buy and use a child, then discard them as if they were trash. I started to attend conferences about human trafficking. I began to research organizations that were already fighting for the cause. I committed myself to studying and I became an expert on the subject.

I found an organization called Not for Sale, that had a thriving Denver chapter. I jumped in and was ready, willing and able to do whatever I could. We organized one of the first walks that year. The walk was 2.7 miles for the number of victims trapped in human trafficking at the time. It was held in downtown Denver and became a huge success. Our task force held many events over the year and helped raised money for a great organization. The lady who ran the chapter at the time was stepping down and wanted me to take over her position. I had a huge decision to make. It wasn't just the volunteering, I would also need to spend over three thousand dollars to fly to California for training and a required minimum of forty hours without pay for the volunteer position.

Remember those boys who had bigger plans for my life? It was during this time that my youngest was put in a children's hospital for a few weeks with a rare form of the croup virus, our car was totaled in an accident without sufficient insurance, and the rental house we had was destroyed and abandoned by the renters. Having three young boys at home, running a salon and volunteering forty hours sounded enticing and rewarding, it just wasn't the right decision for that time. That moment closed, and new opportunities opened.

Using all the knowledge I gained, I was able to start speaking at inner-city schools in Denver on human trafficking. I found out that many of our youth are exposed to child sex trafficking on a higher level than initially thought. I would finish a speech, and a girl would walk up to me and say she was sure her friend was the victim of the boyfriend tactics I had just talked about. It was gratifying to be bringing awareness to the youth, and I really felt that I was making a difference.

I would talk to everyone I met about human trafficking. Almost everyone I explained the world of human trafficking to would either be enraged and motivated to act or change the subject and avoid me the rest of night. I was certainly the highlight of dinner parties (and still am, to be truthful, I'm just a little more diplomatic now). I would talk about it so much that I inspired the barista at a local coffee shop to change his major to focus on human trafficking. I've always wondered what impact they have made.

Not only did I talk about human trafficking, I also created art to raise awareness. I had my works in different arts shows and collaborated with local artists to bring awareness and raise money to help abolish slavery. I would inspire and encourage everyone I met to use their talents to make a difference. Back then, very few had heard of the term "human trafficking." They definitely did not understand how there are more slaves today than in the days of the transatlantic slave trade. Some had heard about it, but thought it was something that only happened overseas and would never be here in America. The conversations were deep and emotional. I'm so thrilled that today when I speak about human trafficking, most people have an idea of what it is. Raising awareness, if that's all we do, can make a difference.

A few years later, I was at a church meeting and the pastor asked a question: If time and money were not an issue, what would you be doing with your life? I immediately raised my hand with emphasis and made sure he saw me, waving it around like a wild woman (when you're passionate about something that's what you do). He called upon me as if he was not surprised I had an answer.

I announced with confidence that I would end child sex trafficking. The next thing the pastor said impacted me forever. He looked at me earnestly and asked a straightforward question: then why are you not doing that now?

Well, because I didn't have the money or time, of course!

To that, he encouraged me and said —if that is what I was called to do, and I wanted it more than anything else in the world, the money and time would manifest themselves. That statement sat with me for a long time. Could I accomplish anything I wanted to achieve? With the right will and focus, could anything be possible?

A month later, the church announced it was going to be taking a few people to India to work with girls born in brothels. The trip cost $10,000 and would be two weeks away from work and family. I was determined to go, but we were still struggling financially, and life was just as crazy as before. I submitted this insane idea to my husband, and he agreed that I should go. It was a miracle in the making. I hosted a showing of a human trafficking movie at my house to raise funds. I hustled and hustled, writing fundraising letters, making phone calls, talking to anyone who would listen and more. I couldn't miss this opportunity to go and see firsthand what life is like in India and in the brothels. I ended up raising twice the amount I needed and was able to gift the orphanage rescuing the girls with a big donation.

India was magnificent with all the colors, smells and cultural differences. Our team traveled all over the southern part of the country and we met some of the most amazing people. The food was also terrific. My favorite was the coffee. They take two separate cups, one with steamed milk and the other with hot coffee, then they raise the cups high over their heads, pouring one into the other. It was a glorious sight and even better on the taste buds.

As a tradition, you eat with your hands, and the delicious food filled with curry and spices is displayed on a banana leaf. I was told to eat with my left hand, which was different and unusual for me being right-handed. I was informed that it's an old tradition there because you wipe yourself with your right hand and, therefore, would not eat with the same hand you wipe with. Fair enough, I thought.

Everything in India is painted in bright, beautiful colors. But behind those amazing colors is a sad truth: many are still oppressed by the Dalit system. Even though it's supposed to be eradicated, the past holds on. Many still believe that the position in life they have been given is theirs forever. If they accept their position with grace, then, upon death, they may come back with more wealth and a higher status in the next life.

In my humble opinion, it is keeping too many in suffering. The system is corrupt, and a few of those in high positions exert their power to rape women. Police raids come in, and many are left without. For the untouchables, they are not allowed to own homes or belongings. I saw streets lined with homeless families sleeping in trash-filled curbs. The babies were just laying there next to mom and dad as cars, carts, and rickshaws missed them by inches. The opportunity to do better, be better, and excel in life isn't even a thought or possibility for those deemed untouchable.

When we visited the orphanage, I met the most amazing children with contagious smiles. We held babies who were on their death beds from malnutrition, and we did crafts and danced with children who have experienced too much pain in the past. We dug ditches, so they didn't have to walk through urine on their way to school. And then we listened, laughed, cried, and loved them.

It was during chapel one day that the girls started to share their stories. These girls were rescued out of the brothels and placed into this orphanage; their mothers were owned by the brothels. Life in a brothel as a child is hard to comprehend. They were made to sleep and play under the very the beds their mothers served clients on daily. Men would rape and abuse their mothers as they stayed utterly still under the bed, praying they were invisible and imagining that they were somewhere else.

Until one day the brothel owner decided that this small child was desirable and ready to be used for sex. Now this child would be raped over and over again. This is the life of many children born in the brothels.

My heart sank, and tears flooded my eyes. I couldn't imagine such an experience. Even more, how could it be that this is the same child I was just singing and dancing with? The same child that has so much gratitude and joy. How was it that this little girl could even smile after living through all that? From their stories, I found my passion and mission: to tell these little girls they are loved, and that they can be anything they want to be. That they could go after their dreams.

I left India understanding what pure joy looks like and knowing that there is no amount of suffering that can ever take our joy, gratitude and happiness. Living in pure joy is a choice that we must make. My desire to help these girls create a new life when they leave the orphanage burned inside of me. Many would age-out and be forced to live on the streets again. They needed education and skills to learn how to survive on their own. They needed someone to believe in them. They needed a system in place that was for them, not against them.

Coming back from India was not an easy adjustment. I heard it's prevalent for there to be an adjustment period after experiencing such poverty, I just wasn't prepared for it. All the things that I used to complain about didn't seem that bad anymore. On the contrary, everything I had now seemed unbelievably beautiful and abundant. The stained carpet I swore needed to be replaced, the granite counter tops I wished were marble, and the couch that lost its support all suddenly looked like the best things in the world. I came home with a new appreciation for what I had. Then dinner time came around.

I decided to make my children a fantastic meal, but it was not received in the same manner as those orphan children. The orphans graciously ate their egg and rice, did their own dishes, and thanked everyone for providing them with food. My children complained about what I cooked, wanted something else, and left their plate for me to clean. I didn't understand how my children who seem to have everything could be so unsatisfied. How could my children who have been provided with clean clothes, a beautiful home, and lots of toys complain so much and be unhappy so much of the time? It wasn't just that either. I would go to the grocery store and get so overwhelmed at the choices we have. I would listen in disbelief as other moms talk about their champagne problems: how the valet parking was taking forever, the massage they just received cut into their day and why someone would bring such cheap wine to the party.

Coming back was a big adjustment and contemplating all that I witnessed in India took some time. It was hard to not yell at times. I wanted to scream at my friends and tell them how inconsequential all of their first-world problems were.

Didn't they know that little girls were being raped daily, hiding under beds and scraping for food? How dare they sit there in their name brand workout clothes, sipping their non-fat lattes, oblivious to the rest of the world. How dare I be right there with them, joining them, enjoying me life. It was a very hard adjustment to come back into my life and be surrounded with so many good things. I had to take a deep breath and remind myself that they don't know because they have never experienced what I had.

Most Americans have never seen the things I have. It wasn't my job to judge or make them understand. I couldn't judge them, or myself, for living a good life. This good life we are living can be used to help those without. I was to celebrate with them and with myself the success we have attained and the lives we have created, so that we can use our wealth and influence to make a difference.

Shortly after returning from India, a book came into my life that changed the way I was fighting human trafficking. It was called Three Cups of Tea, by Greg Mortenson. It was about a mountain climber who unwittingly discovered how to make a lasting economic impact and promote peace. When I read the book, my heart leaped for joy, the clouds parted, and all was right with the world once again. I felt that his ideas on educating and empowering women was what I needed to fight human trafficking. The idea birthed a belief in my heart that if I could end poverty, I can eradicate most of human trafficking. By, educating women and empowering them, we could prevent human trafficking from even starting. This idea could be used to empower girls after they have been found and re-located by an organization to start a new life.

According to Three Cups of Tea, and from what I have seen around the world, when you empower the men, they leave to find a better life. In Africa and other societies, it's common for a man to have multiple wives. When a man leaves, many women are left in extreme poverty and having to start all over. Many have dedicated their lives to raising their children and have not been educated or given the skills to be without support. I have had many conversations with women around the globe about this very issue. Even in America, we have the First Wives Club. It's an unfortunate statistic that just about every culture experiences. Men tend to have more education and knowledge on creating wealth and providing support, leaving the women vulnerable and at risk of being manipulated and trafficked. But if we lend our efforts to empowering and educating women, the women stay and pour into the next generation. We could shape societies to be empowered.

Armed with these new-found ideas and my entrepreneurial skills, I came up with a plan to solve the world's poverty problem. I would start helping women make money while educating them on how to be safe and not fall prey to human trafficking. Again, I started looking for other organizations doing this. I came across this life-changing concept called a micro-loan. My mission was expanding, and ideas were being birthed about how I could change the world and make a difference.

Shortly thereafter, I set out for Africa to help a friend with the same focus. In Uganda, many have been displaced. Entire villages have become the survivors of the LRA (Lord's Resistance Army), and its leader, Joseph Kony, baring scars from the pain he inflicted. Many were forced to kill their own families. Women were raped and mutilated, and boys were rewarded with child sex slaves for every kill.

The violence started in 1987. There are said to be over 1.7 million displaced people groups in Africa who fled from Kony and his war. We went to Africa to help spread love and empowerment. My husband and children were gracious and let me leave again for two weeks to go to yet another country. I went about fundraising and collected enough to make this dream a reality. My heart was set on seeing women set free and empowered. I wanted to see what type of impact could be made by coming alongside those who have been saved from sex trafficking and believing in them, teaching them the skills they need to rise above poverty. Was my idea crazy? Would it really work? I would soon find out.

When I arrived in Africa, I was shocked. I've always pictured Africa a certain way in my mind. First, I thought it looked like a barren desert everywhere you look. What I found in Uganda were lush, beautiful trees and flowing hills. The other misconception I had about Africa was that the country was in need of help. I guess everyone else thought the same thing, because there was a non-profit organization stationed on every corner.

An abundance of NGO's (Non-Governmental Organizations) offering help was everywhere I looked. I soon came to find out that used clothing from America gets shipped over to "help" those in need. The donated clothing is sold at the docks to business owners who then resell it, which in return, puts all those who make clothes and shoes out of business. It was hard to believe these well-meaning non-profits came to Africa to help, but some of their efforts were actually hurting the country. I kept thinking there has to be another way.

While in Africa, I was called a "Mzungu" by the locals, which I didn't mind. It's a fun word Africans call white foreigners. But what I learned next broke my heart and created an even deeper desire for change in me. We were working in the slum areas, and many would call out "Mzungu" with their hands out. Well-meaning foreigners had taught this generation that the Mzungu has the money and they come to give their money. I started asking around about this idea, and what other opinions were on the subject. I started asking questions about why so many non-profit agencies needed to be here. I began to wonder if we broke a society by coming in with our big ideas, deep pockets, and pride. I later found out I wasn't the only one concerned by the cause and effect of going in and taking over a society.

Another book was recommended to me called, When Helping Hurts by, Steve Corbett and Brian Fikkert. It talks about the disservice we can do to a community by moving in, taking over and creating systems how we believe they should be done. There is a saying that if you give a man a fish, he will be fed for a day; teach a man to fish and you will feed him for a lifetime. The living proof of this adage was right in front of me. Didn't these precious people of Uganda know that they did not need the Mzungu to come in and fix their problems by giving them money? They have the power to rise above, and the ability to pour life and wealth into their own communities for future generations. Africa does need clean water, wells, and advocation. It also could use a little less of us doing it all and a little more of us standing beside them with encouragement and belief.

While I was in Africa, I believed more and more in my idea to make a lasting impact on fighting human trafficking by combating poverty through empowerment. I got to work with the most amazingly beautiful women, teaching them and helping them grow their struggling businesses into flourishing ones. I listened and learned how they were selling these paper beads at the Friday market. I experienced their culture and how traditions made it almost impossible to save money. I listened to their stories of hardship and started to understand why they were stuck in this cycle of poverty. Many people were forced into doing things they would never do otherwise do because of poverty, lack of clean water, and dying children.

This is how many end up becoming victims of human trafficking. A mother will stare into the eyes of her starving child, and then a stranger comes by and offers hope. The stranger promises to look after her child, and the child will have a great life and go to school. Desperate for what the stranger is promising to be true, these mothers hand over their child to this so-called "savior." They do not know or understand that this person will turn the child into a slave.

After I learned the struggles and mishaps of why their businesses were not successful, we went to work. I taught a color class. Most of their customers were Western women who liked to shop and bring gifts back from their trips. I explained to them how to put colors together that would appeal to a Western woman. We taught them budgeting skills, as many had no idea if they were making a profit or not. We tried to help them within their social boundaries. It was a custom in their society that when someone asked for money you gave it to them. This would leave them without cash to run their business. We came up with an idea to have different pots of money. Each jar would act as a savings account for the different needs that come up in their lives. Money to buy the paper beads, fix their homes, meet medical needs and to give. When the pot of money to give was out, they could honestly say, "I have no more money to give." We didn't try to change their culture, just help them be empowered and make wise decisions.

I came back from Africa so excited knowing that I could use entrepreneurship as a tool to prevent human trafficking. It was exhilarating, what once was just an idea was now a method that could be used. Praise reports came in on how refugees and survivors of the LRA were using what we taught them to change their lives and break free from a horrible cycle of poverty.

My focus became clear and my mission even clearer. I needed to bring about healing, empowerment, and equip the people to end human trafficking. I could use my story of desperation, abuse and healing to bond with those who have also come from painful past. I could use my story of how I went from standing in welfare lines and being homeless to now being able to help provide support for my family. I found my place in this fight.

I continued to raise support, awareness and work with multiple organizations that were on the front lines of human trafficking. I worked with the Denver University Task Force and helped brainstorm ideas that would impact the industry. I learned that you have to be very careful on how you define and create terms because it could affect the laws being made. I found out that there were more laws against the girls than for the girls I was trying to help and rescue. As time went on, organizations would come and go; volunteers and directors would change often. But my mission remained the same: do as much as I can with the time and resources I had.

Things started to shift in my life for a little while. There was a period of time that raising awareness, joining in on a walk, or giving was all I could do. One of my kids began to struggle, and my focus was directed to getting my child the help they needed. I started to wonder if I should have even taken up this mantle. Was it because I was fighting human trafficking that my family was struggling? Was I not supposed to be doing this? Questions flooded my mind asking why God would ask our family to walk through such a difficult season. I asked God he brought me out of my past life only to be thrown into another season of grief and pain.

Things got really hard on the home front, and some days I could barely hold it together. My mission was shifting. My season of being full-time abolitionist was put on hold. It was also during this season that I got my real estate license and started my new company. Going from a stylist to a real estate agent was a big adjustment. Even through this season of re-focus and struggle I never once stopped sharing the devastation of human trafficking to anyone that would listen.

Friends, let me tell you something: you do not have to fight human trafficking all of the time. You don't have to be on top of your game all the time, start a non-profit, move to another country in order to make an impact. There is so much for you to do right in your own backyard. Life brings us all types of trials and battles to embrace. It's just being open and willing to be there when someone needs you. You don't have to give up your lifestyle, cars, vacations, and homes to make a difference. When the opportunity presents itself, just say, "YES." Even in the midst of your battle, you can help. A small act of kindness goes a long way.

One night a friend called me and told me that they knew someone whose daughter was a victim of human trafficking; they had gone to the police but they were unable to act fast enough. I suggested calling the human trafficking hotline. The hotline helped the mother get in contact with an private detective that finds girls. The mom explained how she had been following her daughter on social media and knew where she is. But if they didn't get her tonight, she would be moved and lost once again. It was a crazy night of phone calls and standing by, at the end of which, I received a phone call thanking me for calling the hotline and for helping to recover that young girl.

I couldn't believe it. Because I talked about human trafficking so much, someone reached out to me for help. It was the perfect chance to put what I was teaching to the test. I called the hotline, and a girl was united back with her mother. That's my hope for this book: that you see how easy it is to make an impact. Just knowing about the cause and being available to help can make all the difference.

The season came that I started to dream again. I had gotten through the worst part with my children. They were safe and happy once again. Kids should come with a warning label:

"Warning: this child may be explosive, unstable, demanding and unpredictable. And double warning: the terrible two's is nothing compare to the teenage years. Do not use all your energy keeping the house clean. You will need that energy later in life."

It's funny because it's true. The fact is that life sends us all kinds of curveballs. Even my friends with fur babies end up with unwanted hospital bills and concern. Sometimes life just beats you down. Dreams you once had are put on a shelf for safe keeping. The problem arises when they have been there so long that they become dusty and forgotten. If you were once in this battle and found that you have lost your passion, or if life has left you exhausted, I'm here to tell you that you are not alone. We must fight together. When one of us needs to rest and regain strength, another one of us will stand in the gap. This is not a battle to be fought alone. Life should not be lived alone. I've seen volunteers come in with zeal and then burn out. It's not a sprint. It's a long-distance generational jog. If you need to step back and focus on other things, do not feel guilty about that. In time you will find your fire again.

I started to get my fire back. I began to embrace my battle and continue on with my mission. I took those dreams of ending human trafficking by fighting poverty, dusted them off and put them back in action. Coming out of difficult years in which I was forged through the fire, made me stronger and wiser. I was ready to re-declare war and use my strength and passion to help others. My mission to heal, empower and equip was back in full force. I found an organization that teaches a business program around the world to end poverty. I partnered with them and went to Nicaragua to help women in prison and other leaders in the community. My youngest son was able to come on this trip with me and see firsthand the poverty in other countries. We visited a feeding center where children walked miles to receive their one meal of the day. My son will forever be impacted by what he experienced and witnessed that day as he served those children their one meal in a dirty container they found.

I feel blessed to have had the opportunity to get to know Emily. She was one of the precious volunteers we were training and is the most amazing missionary I know. She was in her early twenties when she moved to Nicaragua from a small town in the United States to work with the women in prison, many of whom, due to poverty and watching their children starve, made poor choices and were incarcerated. An organization I traveled with called Alternativ teaches missionaries like my friend how to teach a business program. They call the program "Train the Trainers." It equips those on the front lines to teach the business program to the village they are working in. The program is empowering and insightful. It encourages its participants to dream, and then, how to turn that dream into a reality. So many around the world don't even dare to dream. Poverty has a tendency to do that to a person. It sucks all hope out of them and leaves them lifeless. To see someone decide to step out in faith and declare a dream for the first time is priceless. I love to watch the fire grow inside of them and their dignity return, to see their hope restored. The work that we did in Nicaragua will continue on for generations.

As I was preparing for the trip, my ideas and dreams of ending human trafficking were coming together. My vision became clear. We must heal, empower, and equip to restore survivors of human trafficking and prevent more from entering in. Too many times I've heard others say that survivors are too broken and could never overcome the emotional scars to start a business. Countless times I've been told that brokenness is forever. I know firsthand that you can heal from and overcome sexual trauma. You can still have a beautiful family and live a life of dreams. I want to bring emotional healing to these precious souls and show them that they too can be made whole; they too can dream again. There is life after trauma. A beautiful, fulfilling life where anything you can think of or desire can be yours.

As the broken begin to heal and start dreaming again, we must come alongside and empower them, by teaching how to create a profit, handle funds that come in, and multiply them again and again. We must instruct them to be wise, save and invest—things that they may have never heard of before — and teach others to do the same. I believe we can equip people through micro-loans to help them get started on their dreams.

But be aware, not all micro-financing companies are equal. Some charge so much interest that it's just like debt bondage and modern-day slavery. Look at the organization and see what percentage of loans they give are paid back. This will be a good indicator of whether or not the program is working. We want to encourage and empower, not place more bondage upon a person's life.

You must also be careful when supporting organizations that fight human trafficking. There is barely any accountability put in place for these organizations. Anyone can apply for non-profit status and say they are going to work against human trafficking. What a person does after that is not carefully watched. To make a lasting impact, we must demand accountability for those on the front lines. We must give wisely and encourage others to do the same.

I had the privilege to go to Egypt with Alternativ and another organization called, Touch of Love. This trip was special for me because it was the first one that I didn't have to raise funds for, and my business completely supported. I remember the day I wrote the check for over eight thousand dollars and handed it to Lauren, the woman in charge of the trip. It was proof that whatever you want to achieve is possible. It's true, the money and time will manifest themselves in your life. It was also a huge testimony to me that I could rise above, build a legacy and use it to give back. It was a monumental moment in my life. Thinking back about who I was, where I came from and what I had accomplished. I was living proof that you don't have to stay in your pain. There is life after abuse, there is hope after despair. I was proof that a person can overcome sexual trauma and learn to build a business and create a life worth living.

The real estate deal that paid for that trip was a special one, too. It was with some friends of mine who are very dear to my heart. The deal happened to also be one of the more complicated transactions I've ever worked on. It was lined up in such a way that a multitude of things relied on the next. Just one complication, and the whole deal would fall apart. After months of negotiations and moving what at times seemed to be unmovable mountains, it all turned out beautifully. They believed in me and my dreams 100%. I feel this is important for anyone who has a big dream. You need people around you who support you as you go into the battle field. Many of my clients love the fact that I use a portion of my commission to change lives. Many ask how they can help me. At the end of this book you will have many ideas on how you were made to be a part of fighting human trafficking. It will be important for you to share those ideas with others and let them be part of your journey.

In Egypt, I was privileged to witness what a business program equipped with a micro-loan can do to change lives. Egypt is a country with a rich history. It's breathtaking to walk around a country that is referenced in the Bible and history books so often. Just like other countries, there is wealth beyond belief and poverty that breaks my heart. The oppression of women in Egypt was something that I knew existed, but still didn't understand just how it really affected the women there.

For most of my travels, long dresses, being covered up and toning down my makeup was sufficient. So, I packed lots of long dresses, skirts, and scarves. During our sessions, my translator kept commenting on how much she loved my dresses. I just adored her and was even willing to order her one online for all the help she was giving me. I showed her where I got it from and then how easy it was to order her one. Her countenance instantly changed.

She started to tell me that women there don't wear dresses. Being the super curious person that I am, I pressed in, wondering why? I looked around and thought I remembered them wearing dresses, but no, not one local woman was. She started to tell me as tears welled up in her eyes that if you wear a dress or skirt, you will be raped on the way to work. This was not just a story that she was told, it came from personal experience—I could see it in her eyes and the way she explained the story. She assured me that because I was a foreigner, they would not treat me like this; they need tourism, so I would be safe. This broke my heart. All these women live in fear every day of being attacked on the streets. Like so many countries where women's rights are yet to be acknowledged, behavior like this becomes the social norm.

While we were there, we visited the Garbage City in the outskirts of Cairo. On the way there, a graveyard was pointed out to us. Within the tombs, the homeless had set up camp and were living among the dead. Once we arrived at Garbage City, the smell was overwhelming. Imagine heat with rotten garbage and those living among it all mixed together. It's a place where a migrated population have settled. They live among the dump and sort through the trash to find items to sell or recycle. Many of the people have become ill, and children are born with defects from living among the waste.

I had the privilege to visit many different projects where micro-loans are making a difference in the community. We walked through a long alley to met a precious young lady who had been given a micro-loan a few years back. Lining the alley were trash bags stacked high above. People were sitting on top of the trash bags, hauling more bags on their backs or sorting through them. My first instinct was to cover my nose with my scarf. The smell was so repugnant that it was making my stomach turn. I resisted the urge; these beautiful people live here, and I didn't want to offend them.

We entered in through some gates, and before us were two gated stalls with pigs and trash in them. Sitting there amongst the trash was a beautiful lady with a welcoming warm smile. As we approached she got up from where she was sorting trash and greeted us with a warm smile. She was so excited to greet our host and tell her story of how the micro-loan that Touch of Love had granted her was making a difference in her life. I was told when our host first met her, she wouldn't look him in the eye and was ashamed. Time after time he would come to visit, and she would refuse to meet strangers because of embarrassment. Today before us was a very different woman. A woman who was proud and confident, full of joy. With great pride, she told us how she took her first loan to buy materials to help her work more efficiently sorting the trash. She was able to move the garbage out of the tiny room she slept in and rent out this pig stall. She was then able to buy pigs to help dispose of the trash she could not use. She even had hired some of her family to work the business. She paid off the first loan and was able to apply for another loan which she used to expand her business.

I was in awe. My American mind had so many questions about why they choose to stay there, and how this all came to be, a society that lives in the dump. In every developing country I have visited there is a displaced people group living amongst the trash and it breaks my heart. Yet, in the midst of the smell, poverty, and hardship, she found self-worth, purpose, and joy.

I was able to tour many places of business and hear incredible stories just like this beautiful lady's. Where women had nothing, and through training and a small loan, were able to find dignity again, to see hope where there was none. What I witnessed was hope by empowering others to provide for themselves and have pride in what they have accomplished.

There is proof out there that empowerment can lead to changing whole social and economic systems. If we target impoverished areas that have high numbers of human trafficking victims, we could eradicate human trafficking altogether. By bringing healing and business programs, we can impact lives for generations to come. Then, by empowering through a micro-loan, we can give life to dreams that were once buried deep. Hope renewed, dignity restored, people groups empowered. My story won't end here. My vision to see those affected by human trafficking to receive healing, empowerment and equipping will continue to grow and expand.

I hope this book will encourage you to believe that no matter what season of life you are in, there is a place for you in this fight. I will be diving deeper into practical ideas on how you can become an abolitionist in your community and around the world. Whether you are a stay at home mom, white or blue-collar worker, wealthy, or still living with your parents, you too can make an impact. You don't have to fly around the world, give a ridiculous amount of money or give up your day job. There is a place for everyone in this fight.

I started off hosting movie nights to raise awareness. I would tuck my small children into bed and bring out the popcorn. Strangers that I just met would gather in my quaint apartment to watch and learn about human trafficking. As my children grew, I branched out into speaking and running groups. Now, that they are launching out and creating their own lives, my mission is expanding and growing even more.

Remember, nothing in your past can keep you from achieving your goals.

What gifts do you have that you can share? What time do you have to give? Just the littlest thing can make a huge impact. In the next few chapters I will be diving deeper into what human trafficking is, what sex trafficking looks like in the United States, and most importantly, what you can do to create change. This was my story. Your story will look different. We all have a unique path to take. I hope my messy, crazy story gave you hope that you can make a difference. If I can find a way to create change, so can you.

NOTES

NO PEN CAN GIVE AN ADEQUATE
DESCRIPTION OF THE ALL-PERVADING
CORRUPTION PRODUCED BY SLAVERY.
-HARRIET ANN JACOBS

CHAPTER TWO

2 What is human trafficking?

The world is ever evolving, and as technology evolves with it, so does crime. In the early 70's, the war on drugs began with President Nixon declaring that drug abuse was public enemy number one. Let's be honest, the cartels who distributed the drugs were just as much to blamed as the substances and those who used them. Today we are waging a new war with the same players. Whether it's the mafia, mob, or another organized crime system, it seems that there will always be someone in history that will use extortion to get what they want. More now than ever before, with the advancements in technology, crime can hide in the shadows just about anywhere it pleases.

We are declaring a new war in this decade. A battle cry against human trafficking. Those who use extortion and violence to create wealth are expanding through tools like the internet, social media, and drug rings to find, buy and sell human lives. The cartels realized that they can only sell a product like drugs one time, but a young girl they can sell over and over again.

The life expectancy of someone trapped in sex slavery is four years. Once a slave has served their purpose and become no longer of value, that precious human life is disregarded like trash. It doesn't seem to bother the traffickers, there are plenty of girls to be used. The lack of value for human life abounds with those who run enterprises and want to cut production cost. There is no value placed on human life, only on the bottom line. If it means cutting costs and increasing profit, companies look the other way and close their eyes to the abuse that is happening. Shareholders are happy, and profits are flowing in.

This is our new war and a battle cry we must take up. The next generation will have to start pushing back and creating a new revolution. Human lives must matter. We must be aware of what is going on around us. In our suburbs, cities, nation and around the world. We are all connected. Human trafficking is slavery. There are more slaves today than ever before in history. We must answer the call to arms and become equipped to defend our nation.

In just the last decade, I have seen considerable strides towards awareness on this issue. When I first became involved, our primary battle was explaining what human trafficking is. It was a daunting task to have to describe the details of human trafficking before I could even go into how to create an impact. Let's take a moment to celebrate the monumental impact that has been made by shedding a light of awareness on this evil's existence. The truth is, knowing is half the battle. By bringing such injustice into the light and educating others, we are moving mountains, and it is just the first step in a long uphill battle. How can we defend against an enemy if we do not understand who we are fighting?

The fact that you picked up this book, made it through the introduction, my story, and are still with me means something must be stirring inside of you. Somewhere inside you, there is an understanding that we cannot sit by and do nothing when there is so much hurt and pain in this world. We cannot look the other way when a person would treat another— especially a child — in such inhumane ways, and precious individuals' rights are taken from them.

We've made significant strides and movements in the past. With segregation ending in the 60's and the equality movement of the 80's, one would hope and believe that we have moved past slavery as a country. It's time for another movement and revolution, one where we cry out that human trafficking (modern-day slavery) shall end.

Laws are changing daily. More victims are being identified, and justice is being served. It's my goal to give you the most up to date information and definitions I possibly can. Many things have changed over the past decade since I've become an abolitionist. I'm expecting and hoping they will keep changing in the right direction. A few years ago, a girl as young as eleven could be convicted of prostitution. This blows my mind. I never could understand how the laws could allow an eleven-year-old to go to jail for this type of crime.

By working on the definitions, telling the survivors stories, and raising awareness, we can set the captives free. My goal is to teach you how to stay aware and educated—to use this book as a guide on how you can get involved. But it's just a foundation to build on. If you are intrigued and moved by something in this book, I urge you to dig deeper until you fully understand the problem. Knowledge is power. With the power of awareness, we can overcome and change the course of history.

But to win the battle against human trafficking, we must first understand what we are up against. We must learn what it is, what it looks like, who our enemy is and how we can make an impact. This next chapter will give you a very brief understanding of what human trafficking is and what it looks like. This chapter will be going over the global issues of human trafficking. In the following chapter I will focus on child sex trafficking in America.

Let's get started.

The term human trafficking can be defined as simply as: modern-day slavery.

The dark truth is that slavery still exists. There are more slaves today than there were during the transatlantic slave trade. Instead of slave ships holding up to 600 slaves chained and shackled, we now have websites where men, women, and children are being traded like a commodity.

If you are like me, you may have thought that we have already won the fight against slavery. Starting with Slavery Abolition Act of 1833. Forerunners like Harriet Tubman, Freedom Riders, and Martin Luther King paved the way for a new way of thinking and acceptance. Just thinking about the heroes of the past gives me chills. Thinking of the courageous acts of these heroes fills me with excitement and hope for the future. Today we are making history. The next generation of heroes *will* rise. It could be you.

As we raise awareness and more and more people understand what human trafficking is, what it looks like and who it is affecting, we can start making a lasting impact. This starts by identifying victims. Many are still not being identified as victims—mostly due to the laws and how we define human trafficking. The more we understand how individuals get entrapped the more we can help create systems to free them.

Laws

When I first became involved in the movement against child sex slavery, there were more laws against the children we were trying to save than for them. The definitions we use can create laws to rescue or harm the very victims we are trying to help. As I am going into the definitions and different ways people are becoming slaves, keep in mind that your place in all of this may be advocacy. If you're feeling pulled to start a non-profit, speak to a group, or organize a run, the words you use can help or harm the very people you try to help. Those of us fighting human trafficking are up against a long roll of red tape holding up grants, democracy, and change. Some wonderful organizations have dedicated their lives to learning these laws and lobbying for them to be restructured to help victims.

Human trafficking is modern-day slavery. This is an accurate and easy answer to a very complicated, dark web that is being spun in the most secret and open places. Modern-day slavery can take form in many different ways. There are thirty-four definitions of human trafficking, and the FBI acknowledges at least *twenty-five* of them. It can be very complicated trying to sort out and understand what it all means.

Let's start with the UNODC (United Nations Office on Drugs and Crime) who provides a very long definition for human trafficking:

> Article 3, Paragraph (a) of the Protocol to Prevent, Suppress, and Punish Trafficking
> in Persons defines Trafficking in Persons as the recruitment, transportation, transfer, harboring or receipt of persons, by means of the threat or use of force or other forms of coercion, of abduction, of fraud, of deception, of the abuse

of power or of a position of vulnerability or of the giving or receiving of payments or benefits to achieve the consent of a person having control over another person for the purpose of exploitation. Exploitation shall include, at a minimum, the exploitation of the prostitution of others or other forms of sexual exploitation, forced labor or services, slavery or practices similar to slavery, servitude or the removal of organs.

Phew! That was complicated. You may have just glazed over while reading that until it got to the end and the words "prostitution" and "removal of organs" showed up. That got your attention for sure.

You may need a little more clarification, such as, what is a trafficker and who would be paying for these people? What does all this mean anyways?

A human trafficker is the person who is getting paid or compensated for what another person did. It could be a pimp selling another person for sex and keeping the money, or a business owner having someone work for them and not giving them adequate pay or working conditions.

Another definition that will come up is a "John." This term is used to describe a man who is buying another person to use them for sexual acts.

But what about the other stuff? What are we really talking about? Slavery, sex, and organ removal? Can this all be real or is it just the script from a Liam Neeson movie? I'm going to break it down, starting with the easiest for me to handle emotionally and working my way to the worst, most horrible, gut-wrenching scenarios. Scenarios that have kept me up at night praying over how these little lives can be saved.

There are a few general types of human trafficking: labor and commercial trafficking, forced marriage, child brides, human organ trafficking, sex trafficking, familial trafficking and child sex trafficking. As awareness spreads and education widens, we are becoming more and more aware of different ways people are being entrapped as slaves, and therefore, better equipped to liberate them.

Labor Trafficking

In the early 2000's, we were stating 2.7 million slaves trapped in human trafficking. According to the International Labor Organization, 40 million people were victims of modern day slavery in 2016. As of 2017 they are reporting that 24.9 million people are trapped in forced labor. Why such a big jump in numbers over a decade? What in the world is happening, and why are we not making an impact? I believe that awareness and exposure have finally made us realize just how many slaves there are and how many are being affected. But don't lose hope, that's why you are reading this book: to be educated and empowered to change the world.

I just love that quote from the animated series, *Pinky and the Brain*:
"What would you like to do tonight, Brain?"
"Same thing we do every night, Pinky. Try to take over the world."

Let's do that!
Let's take over the world and end slavery.

That is the majority of modern-day slaves.

What is labor trafficking? It is when an employer or person makes false promises, uses force, fraud, deception, abuse of power, abduction or other means to lure people into horrible, unethical working conditions. Sometimes parents are selling their children to these traffickers. But many times people are desperate enough for work and money that they will go willingly with anyone promising a job at the other end. When they get there, they realize they have been deceived.

The person who is enslaved makes no money at all or they are severely underpaid. They are being held against their will and have no way of escaping. It often looks like a person who was brought or smuggled into the country with the promise of a job, and now finds their passport and all records taken from them. They don't know anyone or speak the language, and they can't go to the officials of that country because they are in that country illegally. The trafficker is taking full advantage of this individual knowing they are trapped. Another way labor trafficking presents itself is in the form of debt bondage.

Debt bondage is when someone is hired to do a job— let's say work a field —and when they arrive, they are told that they will be charged for the travel to the worksite. This money is then deducted from their pay. Then they find out, to be able to do their job, they must rent tools—that is also deducted from their pay. If they want food, water, housing or just about anything else, that too is deducted from their pay. Now these trusting souls owe more money than they make, and they are told they must pay it back. There are documented cases of generations being forced to "work off" their grandparents' debt of being brought into that country. It becomes a never-ending cycle, and it is slavery. This is very common in developing countries but can be found all over the world — the United States included. In India, there are cases of debt bondage in the brick kilns, where families and children are forced to work off a debt that keeps increasing. If they try to run away, they are caught and locked in a room with no food or water, where they are beaten or deprived of basic human needs.

Here are a few examples of what this looks like in real life. Documented cases in Colorado have exposed to the world how immigrant sheepherders are being abused. These precious souls are promised a better life and transported from Peru and surrounding areas. Once they are here, the job they thought they were signing up for in the land of freedom turns out to be not very free. Passports and Visas are taken if they had any, and they are forced to work long hours and live in a small trailer with no running water or heat. One case found forty men cramped into one small trailer. With no ability to speak English and no transportation, they are hidden far west in the mountains, out of reach of civilization. Violence, verbal abuse, restriction of food, and other human rights violations are used to keep them in line.

In the Nepal kilns, there are many cases of children under the age of fourteen being forced to work in harsh conditions making bricks. Women and men who were tricked or forced into working in these conditions find themselves enslaved. Hazardous conditions create lifelong health conditions, burned limbs, lack of medical care and more.

In Spain, there was a bust that resulted in 180 arrests and many lives saved. Women were being forced to work in a factory, barely clothed and only allowed a few hours of sleep a night with their mattress in the same room where they ate and used the bathroom. Sexual abuse was used as a punishment.

That operation was busted by just *one* complaint. Did you hear that? Read it again, let it sink in. *One* complaint. All it takes is one call, one person willing to take a chance to save the lives of those who cannot speak for themselves. This one complaint took three years to amount to the arrests and the operation shutting down. Three years is a long time to wait for something to happen, but now the men and women who were responsible for those crimes will never be able to harm another soul again. Justice was served.

Forced Marriage

Growing up in America, I was raised on movies like *Aladdin* and *Brave*. Both films are about young girls forced to marry someone they do not know or love. Like many American girls, I grew up with visions of a princess who must marry for politics and not love. In those fairytales, it ends with them finding their prince and everlasting love. Unfortunately, life is not like the fairy tales. There are religions out there that allow and encourage the marriage of multiple young wives and even child brides. It goes across countries, cultures, and beliefs. In some cultures—like Ethiopia—there are rituals where the young child's female genitalia will be cut or mutilated as a passage into womanhood. In cultures of poverty, girls may be sold as brides to help their family financially.

According to Girls Not Brides, there are 12 million girls married before the age of 18 every year. That's 23 girls every minute! When can a child bride be considered a human trafficking victim? When the marriage of that girl profited someone else. Parents benefit by marrying their child off to the highest bidder. What also occurs because child marriage is still legal in many areas of the world, is that the person who marries the child does so with the intention to get around the laws. They marry the child bride and then sell them for sex, and now it becomes child sex trafficking. The problem with child marriage—besides the obvious—is that many of these girls don't get the opportunity to go to school, they are abused and subjected to horrible conditions, and they sometimes become the fourth or fifth brides of this man. Many become slaves, not beloved wives.

Organ Trafficking

There are usually three different ways that people fall prey to organ trafficking: they go in for a medical procedure and then find that one of their organs was taken without their consent; they sell their organs for money, only to find that the terms changed, and they never get paid; or they get forced into giving their organs. The kidney is the most common organ to be trafficked. The waiting list is long, and the legally attained organs available do not meet the current need. There are urban legends about people who are drugged at parties and wake up in a tub of ice with a note next to them that says to seek medical attention. *Yikes!* That sounds horrifying. Fortunately, it's not that common, but it still happens.

Writing a book about stomach-turning social injustices and human rights violations is not easy. But by shedding light on and recording everything that I have experienced, witnessed and learned over the last decade with pen and paper, I'm hoping that even just one of you will be inspired to make a difference, raise a voice and create the change we need to see in this world. I hope that just one of you will be more careful when you go out to the clubs, bars, or travel. I don't want to strike fear into your hearts. I just want to raise awareness that such things happen, and with purposeful intention, we can educate others to stop these violations from happening as often. It could be that this book inspires one of you to invent a small stick or straw that you keep in your glass to test for toxins, or some other safety device. You must message me if anything in this book inspires you. I want to hear all of your stories of how you are fighting against human trafficking.

The most common human trafficking cases are due to individuals taking advantage of others who are impoverished or hurting. Those who are hungry are also desperate for hope and change. When you have no other options, it's almost impossible to say no to an individual that is offering you something that looks like a way to survive. This is why I fight so hard to bring more education and empowerment to those who are struggling to survive. I believe education and empowerment can reduce human trafficking. If more people were less frightened about what tomorrow will bring, and empowered to create an income, fewer people would fall prey to human trafficking. By educating individuals on how others may approach them and offer false hope, we can stop abuse from happening. Too many who cannot feed their families find themselves in a bad situation. Those who are fighting to live tend to go against common sense in exchange for hope. The more we shed light on these situations, the less injustice can happen. When you turn on a light switch in a dark room, the darkness no longer exists. You are the light in this world. You have the power to chase out the darkness.

As I go into the next few ways human trafficking can happen, brace yourself. From my experience, sex trafficking cases are the hardest for others to hear about and process emotionally.

Sex Trafficking and Child Sex Trafficking

< *Deep Breath* >

That night at the movies when I first realized that child sex trafficking existed is a moment in time that I will never forget. From the smell of the theater to the pain in my heart, the way I could barely catch my breath as I sobbed for the whole theater to hear. It was in that moment that I knew this was my calling, that I must do something, anything, to stop the harm that was being done to these little girls. I didn't know how or where to start, I just knew it had to be done.

This new knowledge penetrated to the core of who I was as a mother. Thoughts of never allowing my children to leave my side, ran through my mind. Obviously, this was not a

43

practical way to raise three boys. Instead of being paralyzed by fear, I choose to walk in faith. I chose to pick up the mantle and fight for their generation—to make a safer world for them.

I would sob every time I thought of those little girls on that film saying they give good "yum-yum." My heart was ripped out from the inside and exposed for the whole world to see. The moment in India when I looked those little girls in the eye as they told me their stories about being born in the brothels, and when a survivor told her story of how she was beaten and raped daily as a child, those are the stories that live with me.

Those are the children that I sobbed over the other day at church when we sang the words,

"every precious child you died to save."

I fell to my knees, like a little baby, sobbing and wiping mascara off with my coat sleeve. I was wrecked!

I'm still wrecked, longing for those precious little ones to be protected and saved. How you respond will be different from my story. I just encourage you to not dwell on the ugly, heartbreaking side of this injustice. I encourage you to have hope that little lives are being rescued, renewed and empowered daily. Beautiful people like you have answered the call and lives are being saved. Let this knowledge equip you to make the world a better place.

In another chapter I will dive deeper into child sex trafficking in the United States; it is imperative that I use a whole chapter for you to be genuinely equipped to go and fight human trafficking in your own neighborhoods. If you don't live in the United States, the ideas I present to make an impact remain the same, I feel many Americans have this idea that this injustice does not happen in their country. It does!

My dear fellow Americans, please understand that sex trafficking is a rapidly growing epidemic in the United States, from small towns, big cities and even in the suburbs—everywhere. We all must stand together. The United States needs to stand with the rest of the world to fight what is now a global epidemic.

What is sex trafficking? It's when someone is forced by threats, deception, lies, debt bondage, violence, or other methods of coercion to provide commercial sex and sexual acts.

Women, men, girls, boys—no one is safe from this horrible crime that violates a human being in the most profound way.

Reading examples of this atrocity may make your stomach turn but hang in there. Soon we will be shedding light on what you can do to fight for those who cannot speak for themselves. In just a few chapters, I will be giving you the power to take up the mantle and bring justice to these survivors. Hope is coming.

How do I even begin writing out all these horrific crimes? I've read so many books that describe these events in detail that they are scarred into my heart forever. Do I explain it in such a way that you have nightmares, and the tears of those little ones' hurt become your tears? Or do I glaze over it and just give you an overview? It is my hope that I'm able to tell their stories in such a way as to empower you.

Sex Tourism

Yes, this is a real thing. When I first heard about it, I was shocked. Sex tourism is where men—and some women—travel to another country for the sole purpose of having sex. In many cases it's to have sex with underage girls, sex that is destructive or the like. They are promised that all of their wildest sexual fantasies will be fulfilled. What these men do not know, or do not care about, is that these precious individuals who are being sold for sex are almost always in some type of slavery. They are being held against their will, beaten and drugged into performing. If they don't sexually perform as expected, they will be punished. Their captors threaten to kill or hurt them and their families if they do not comply.

This is happening all over the world. Thailand, Amsterdam, India, and Cambodia are some of the most common breeding grounds for exploitation. In Cambodia, young girls are auctioned off as young as five years old for sexual exploitation. The average client buying these girls are white men, around 40 years old, and make over 70k a year. I will go into this more in the next chapter about how this is fueling sex slavery in America.

Operation Underground Railroad produced an eye-opening documentary on how sex tourism happens and what they are doing to combat it. In the documentary, Tim Ballard, an ex-CIA agent, takes a team undercover into the darkness of sex tourism. They pretend to be big-ballers who are visiting for a bachelor party. They go around and find traffickers who are willing to bring them underage girls as young as 14 so they can have sex with them at a party they are throwing. The good news for these girls is that Tim and his team have no interest in exploiting them like the other men who have requested them in the past. They were there to rescue them. We need more people like Tim and his team who are raising awareness and using their talents to help end child sex slavery.

Prostitution

In every country around the world there is prostitution in some shape or form. The women who are trapped in this industry are hurting and need to be shown love and a way out. The emotional scars of sexual violation tear deep. How did these precious souls get locked behind bolted doors and cages?

It could be that they applied to be nannies, house keepers, models or similar professions. Filled with excitement and hope for their future they took the job planning to send the money home to their families. Once they arrive at these so-called promised jobs, their passports are taken, and with that, all hope. Most are drugged so that their bodies will crave the drugs and do anything to have their fix. Many are beaten, intimidated and raped—even by police officers. It's a psychological attack to show they have nowhere to go. The traffickers let the police officers "break in" the new product free of cost, and in return the police turn the other way.

In developing counties, daughters are sold to travelers passing by, promising to take care of them and give them school in return for being housekeepers. In Nepal, children are kidnapped on their way to school. The traffickers are crafty, making promises they never intend to keep. Virgins go for the highest dollar and are kept secluded until the highest bidder purchases them. They then rape these children, taking the very thing God gave them to give to someone they love, something that can never be replaced.

Violated, abused and shamed, these victims become trapped. Many are forced to service 20-45 men a day as they are being starved, beaten, or mutilated—broken beer bottles shoved up their vaginas or burning cigarettes inside of them.

Many give birth while in slavery, and their children at the ages of 3 and up are expected to perform sexual favors or be used for sexual pleasure.

An organization called Love 146 was formed during a trip to South East Asia. What they found broke their hearts. Young girls kept in glass cages on display for men to purchase for sexual pleasures. They recall going into one brothel and young girls (some as young as 5) came towards them with smiles, offering sexual favors as if asking for candy, jumping up and down encouraging the grown men to buy them.

The documentaries and books I've read on this are heartbreaking. As I write this, tears are flowing. I can still see those girls tugging on the shirts of those men saying they give the best yum-yum and will please them very much. As you may have noticed, this is the scene that stays with me the most. This is the scene that I close my eyes and think of when I want to give up and forget everything I know about child sex trafficking. Those little girls are the ones I am writing this book for.

The founder of Love 146, Rob Morris, went to another brothel and displayed in the glass cases were little girls watching T.V and playing with dolls. Most girls looked like life was taken from them, despair washed over them, all joy gone from them. But not the girl in case 146. She still had fight left in her eyes. So, he left that place and started Love146 for the girl who still had fight in her.

In Victor Malarek's book, *The Natashas*, a man goes undercover to expose the Russian mafia. He explains the horrific scene of women who thought they were going to be famous models, well-paid housekeepers, nannies or something of the like, but when they arrived at their new job, the horrifying truth was revealed. These beautiful girls were now the property of sex traffickers, trapped in sex slavery where they will have to do unimaginable things. These beautiful Russian women who their traffickers referred to as "Natasha" were forced to play out men's most unimaginable, sadistic, sexual fantasies against their will. I have listened to similar stories. I've watched tears flow down their faces as they told me their stories. They did not ask for that life. It was forced upon them.

It's a sad truth that some judge those who are trafficked because of how they became a victim. In many cultures around the world once a girl has been raped, she is called untouchable. She will never be welcomed into her village again. Open your eyes, your mind, and your heart to those suffering. Chances are the person next to you knows all too well what it feels like to have a hand on their thigh that they do not want there. Allow love to enter your hearts and then do something about it. Let's fight for each other. It's time to say, this is not okay.

I'm even going to ask you to find room in your heart for the men who are paying to have sex with these little girls. They struggle with mental illness and addiction. I highly doubt when they were little boys they thought they would rape little girls one day. That's why we need organizations like Shared Hope and doctors like Dr. Doug Weiss to get these men the help they need. We need more organizations that are working with the John's and breaking them free from their sexual addiction. Battling this injustice at the root—with the demand.

This is a battle that needs to be fought on all sides. It cannot be won with hate. Only love can conquer this darkness. Love strong enough for all those involved. Love will be the light that shines so bright in this dark world of human trafficking.

The Other Ugly Stuff

There are so many other ways beautiful souls are sex trafficked. One of the at-risk groups not yet mentioned are the dancing boys of Afghanistan; little boys being sexually abused by other men and forced to dance and perform sexual favors for them.

Unfortunately, there are just really sick people out there who buy other people to torture them for fun. In the book, *A Crime so Monstrous*, Benjamin Skinner talks about a group of flight attendants who purchased a small African boy. They took him to a bathroom stall, had him pull out his penis, and did unthinkable things to him while laughing. There are stories upon stories of people selling other people so that their fetishes can be satisfied and profits made. Stories that remain with me and cannot be removed from my soul. Stories that have fueled me for years to do what I do.

This chapter does not even touch on or cover the whole story of human trafficking. It's a small look into a very dark world that is operating all around us. I would encourage you that if one of these stories moved you, if something resonated deep in your soul, then go and do something about it. Start by reading more books, listening to more speakers, learning all that you can. The more we know, the less these types of human rights violations can happen. The more aware we are of the things going on around us, the harder it is for slavery to hide in plain sight.

Knowledge is power.

NOTES

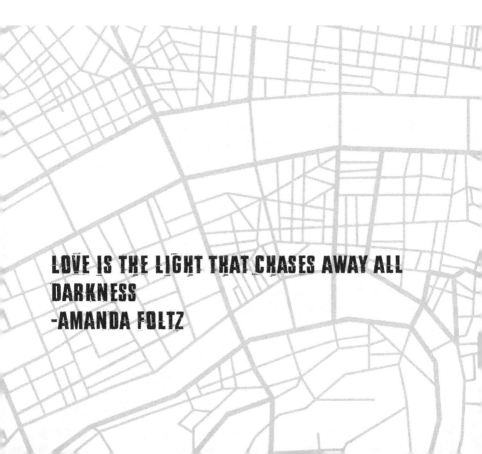

LOVE IS THE LIGHT THAT CHASES AWAY ALL
DARKNESS
-AMANDA FOLTZ

3 CHAPTER THREE
Sex Trafficking in America

3

Every type of human trafficking explained in the last chapter happen in America, and they are growing at exponential rates. I was born and raised in America, and I am shocked at the responses of my fellow citizens when the subject of human trafficking is brought up. Most Americans assume that this is an issue somewhere else. Let's begin our revolution with changing this way of thinking. Everyone must understand that human trafficking is everywhere. No matter what country you live in. No matter the size of your state, city, or community. Understanding and believing that we can come across victims daily is a huge step to abolishing sex trafficking.

Next, we must know how to identify and report these crimes. I can't express how important it is that everyone knows and understands how to identify victims. If all we do is spread the word and tell everyone we know that modern day slavery exists, we will be creating change. Together, we can stand strong and protect our communities and those who live in them.

Imagine what could happen if we decided to become the neighborhood watch in our communities? What if we balanced our efforts between the global crisis and vowing to keep where we live safe, educating our neighbors, schools, chambers, and businesses around us? Imagine a community that has a safe space for victims to come forward and be given the help they need.

As a Realtor, I travel all over the beautiful state of Colorado. I have numerous opportunities to spread awareness through my wonderful state. I also understand neighborhoods and know when something is off about a home or area.

What line of work are you in?

Where do you travel, visit, shop, or play?

What skills can you utilize to fight human trafficking?

Soon you will have an opportunity to think, write and plan out how you can make a difference. As you read this next chapter, start thinking about if you come across these areas in your daily routine. Could there be a victim in your life, on that street you pass daily, next to your place of business, on the way to the gym, kids soccer practice, or favorite coffee shop? When you learn the indicators and understand what human trafficking looks like, it activates your RAS (Reticular Activating System). I could geek out on this all day. Your brain is a powerful tool, and you can train it to identify victims. RAS is when you focus on one thing and then see it everywhere. It's when you buy a new car, and as soon as you drive it off the lot, you start seeing that brand of car everywhere. When we educate ourselves and learn the indicators of human trafficking, your brain will begin finding victims. One day you will be walking down the same street you walk down every day and then, all the sudden, you see a massage parlor that says it services men only. You never thought anything of it before, but now that you know the signs your neurons fire up and tickle your thought process, begging for attention.

Child sex trafficking is something that I am passionate about ending. I talk about it all the time during parties, meetings, events, even in the locker room. At times, I'm a little worried that I have become desensitized to the subject. I also tend to forget how it can affect people when they hear about innocent children being sexually abused and sold into slavery for the first time. I just know that the more I talk about it, I increase my chances of inspiring someone to become the next Rosa Parks. That's why you will find me telling anyone who will listen about the slaves around the world and how we must help rescue them. I am also keenly aware that this is not a subject that some people are comfortable discussing with a complete stranger.

Not too long ago, I dropped my son off at golfing and then went to grab a drink at the bar. The topic came up that I'm currently writing a book, and I was asked what it was about. Yep, the poor guy had no idea what was coming when he asked that question.

I started going into the subject of child sex trafficking, and he just outright said, "I'm not comfortable talking about this." I gave a gentle smile and said that I respect that, then asked him if he had a good golf game and mentioned how beautiful the weather was.

I make things so awkward; you just can't take me anywhere. But I don't care. I have a cause that I can't stop talking about when given the opportunity. At the end of the conversation he did connect me with an organization he knew about that fights human trafficking from a golf fundraiser he went too, and we left it at that.

So, that guy didn't want to hear all about how Denver is on the slave trade, how I70 is a huge slave trade route, or how brothels are popping up in the suburbs. That is why I'm so thankful for all my followers and you. You are reading this book because you want to be equipped to make a difference— whether a small or humongous difference in this world. Give yourself a pat on the back. I'm serious. Reach over and pat yourself on the back. Say, "way to go self. You deserve it. You are a world changer." Just by picking up this book and reading it, you are doing something. I'm going to repeat that. You are truly doing something to change the world by reading this book. Only by understanding what is going on, can we truly start to make a difference.

I hope this book gets in the hands of kind-hearted people all over the world. I pray that this message and awareness spreads like wildfire. I hope my story makes an impact and I will consider this book a success if only one of you goes and implements the ideas in this book. If only one of you tells a friend, if only one of you calls the hotline, if only one of you gives to support your favorite organization. It doesn't take much to create a butterfly effect.

To understand how a majority of children end up as sex trafficking victims, we need to understand what "at-risk" means. You may hear the term being thrown around if you are diving deeper into human trafficking and how to help. The government defines kids who are "at-risk" as those who are being raised in families with economic hardship. Here again is poverty at work. Those who have financial strains or even a lacking support network become targeted. Other kids are deemed at-risk if they display delinquent behaviors such as dropping out of school, running away, using drugs, depression, drinking, fighting, etc. Kids that are being bullied or live in abusive homes. Kids who are in the LGBTQ (lesbian, gay, bisexual, transgender, queer) community are at risk.

In many of the examples in this chapter, the predators will prey on "at-risk" youth and use different methods to entrap them. But don't be fooled, there are plenty of cases of those raised in the upper middle class who become victims as well. Kids living in the inner city are not the only ones at risk. I point this out because I want to dissolve any idea that these crimes do not exist in your community. I'm trying my best to take the blinders off and open your eyes that these crimes operate anywhere and everywhere.

The fact is that anyone can be a victim of human trafficking. Though it is also true that the majority of victims do fall under the "at-risk" profile. There are many ways sex trafficking can operate all around us. I encourage you to read more books and do more research on this subject. Become experts by talking to your local law enforcement, task force, ICE (Immigration and Customs Enforcement) or FBI (Federal Bureau of Investigation) offices. Understanding these tactics will give you a solid foundation to build upon. Let's dive into the different types of sex trafficking that could be operating around you.

Prostitution and sexual exploitation

This is where the laws get tricky, and great organizations like Polaris and International Justice Mission are forerunners on getting the laws restructured to help those trapped in sex trafficking. The majority of prostitutes fall under the blanket of human trafficking.

In human trafficking cases, a pimp, trafficker, aunt, uncle, boyfriend or someone else takes charge of another human being. They start demanding that they serve a set number of clients per day. They use a multitude of different tactics to manipulate and abuse their victims into doing what they want.

I recently saw the movie Pretty Woman. When I first watched it, I wasn't aware of sex trafficking. Now that my eyes are open, the film actually saddens me. It paints this picture of a beautiful young girl who was down on her luck. After a series of mishaps and unforeseen challenges in her life, she was introduced to a girl named Kit who showed her the ways of the streets. In the movie, she was living on the streets on her own terms, meaning she had sex with whom she wanted, when she wanted, implementing rules like not kissing the men on their lips. She even had the luxury of using condoms for protection and floss to keep strawberry seeds out of her teeth. One day a knight in a shiny white limo came to her rescue, and she no longer had to be on the streets; she was given a chance at a life full of love and luxury. Unfortunately for everyone else, life does not work out like that.

No, this is not the life of Pretty Women. This is not 50 Shades of Grey. This is not the women asking for it. This is not their fault. This is not the way some things are. This is not how some women want to live their life, women's choice, or whatever phrases people use to justify this. This is horrific and needs to stop!

There is not a girl in the world that thinks, "gosh, I hope I will be a prostitute when I grow up, and men will pay money to have sex with me." That's why I support organizations that are working with the girls on the streets. Whether these girls fall under human trafficking or not, they all need love. Each one needs someone to say that you are lovable, that they matter. Each one needs to be shown that they are worthy of so much more! They don't need religion shoved in their face or told that they are sinners. They don't need one more person telling them they are horrible, wrong or filthy. They need acceptance and love. Trust me, I know. Maybe you know too. Perhaps you once were abused and felt unlovable, dirty, and unworthy. Those who have been victimized don't need accusers making them feel worse, they just need unconditional love.

It's possible that you can say #metoo with sexual abuse. According to the National Sexual Violence Resource Center they say, 1 out of 3 women, and 1 out of 6 men have been sexually abused or raped. Pause and look around you. How many men and women are around you right now? How about at work, in church, in your life? That number is astounding. Not one woman, child, boy or man ever deserves to be touched in a way that sends chills up their back. No one deserves to be touched in a way they did not concede to, to be exploited and taken advantage of.

In the last chapter, we went over the definitions of sex trafficking and prostitution. Remember, the definition of human trafficking is when someone else is getting paid for the labor or efforts of another person. A prostitute is someone who is paid to engage in sexual activity. When a person is being trafficked, someone else is getting paid for that sexual activity.

Allow me to explain for a moment how many girls end up in horrible situations. Whether they are being trafficked or are lost in the darkness. There are many different stories, reasons and thought processes that bring a girl trapped into this world.

I ended up working in a bikini club with the thought process that it would just be until I got back on my feet. When I heard of sex trafficking, my heart broke. I was so close to becoming entrapped into that world. I pondered questions, asking why I was protected and saved from that world. I was right on the edge. I was first exposed to strip clubs when a group of my military guy "friends" brought me to one, and then encouraged me to get on stage. In that moment, I felt beautiful for the first time in a long time. Though I was only 17, their cheering and applause made me feel wanted and desired. By that point, I had already been raped multiple times. I was slowly losing my voice, and what I wanted was rapidly disappearing. Those experiences were teaching me that that was all I was worth, that my body was all men wanted from me. I started to grow weary of fighting them. It was easier for me to accept this as the sum total of my worth.

I had recently been honorably discharged from the United States Air Force and relocated to Florida to create a new life, and I was determined to make it a better one. When the non-profit I was working at told me there was no money to pay me and bills were due, I went were I knew I would be accepted.

The bikini club, that I drove past everyday on my way to work. I walked into that club and got a second job.

It was thrilling in the beginning. I stopped working at the non-profit and went full-time at the club. I justified it by telling myself that at least I wasn't dancing nude, that it would only be a month or so, it would just be until. . . Insert any number of lies I was telling myself. Many girls get trapped in a life they never intended to live. Just like me, they went somewhere just once for help, only to find that there are really evil people out there that will take advantage of your hard times to manipulate you and trap you. One step into that club and I started to get deeper into a world I did not belong in. It wasn't long until I slowly found myself being controlled by others who had ill intentions for me.

Some of the girls I knew would go and support other dancers at different clubs. When I was visiting a strip club with a friend, I was surprised to find a girl from my high school working there. When I last saw her, she was on her way to be a top model. I remember she would travel to exotic places modeling for magazines. I wanted to be her, every girl in my high school wanted her life. Somehow, she went from top model to stripping for strangers. I know she never said to herself while growing up, "Gee, I really hope that I get to work in a strip club, where a pimp will find me, take my freedom away and then start to sell me!" No, she had big dreams for her life. Somewhere along the way those dreams were smashed, and she slowly found herself lost in a dark world with little hope of getting free.

It was a miracle I was able to escape before reaching the point of no return. The darkness was so close at times, calling out to me. The lies and abuse that I had been trained with told me that's where I belong. The inner struggle was slowly killing me. There are many days that I look back in awe of where I have been and where I am now. I feel so lucky compared to the many stories I've read of girls who end up trapped and owned. Girls who end up losing all freedom, who ended up being trafficked and eventually losing their lives. Those who eventually are set free end up with such deep emotional scars that they never become emotionally free of the abuse done to them. I don't know why I was able to escape. Why me and not them? I do know that those who have been forgiven much, love much. I do know that I will never take my freedom for granted, I plan on using every day I am given as a gift. I may not know the pain of being sold to a multitude of men daily, I may not know what it would ever be like to sleep under a bed while my mother is raped above me. What I do know is that no one should ever know that type of pain. No one should ever have to live like that. Everyone deserves love, kindness and acceptance. As long as this type of evil exists, I will share my story, their stories, and advocate for freedom.

After I was set free and started getting my life renewed, I began helping with offering prostitutes a chance to get off the streets. One of my good friends who finally broke free from prostitution started out thinking it would be a onetime thing. She had been sexually abused as a child and believed that was her worth. She then ended up in an abusive situation when a pimp claimed her as his and forced her to continue with the prostitution life. She eventually broke free from his control, but it wasn't until years later that she broke free from the "call of the streets."

Abuse, the streets, and violence become normal. It takes a miracle to break free from the physiological effects of being on the streets. Victims become accustomed to the abuse. It becomes their new normal. Some girls that I have mentored have come out of trafficking situations only to keep winding up on the streets again. For some, it's all they know. They have been taught since they were very little by family that that is their worth—or it's how they have been taught to survive. Many get trapped in the world of sexual exploitation with no hope of getting out, physically or mentally. Those who are in prostitution are not there because they "want" to be. That is a huge misconception.

Years ago, there was a case of an 11-year-old being convicted of prostitution. Through activism, the laws are changing to protect our children. There is a delicate line in this fight when deciding whether or not the person was acting on their own and should be charged as a prostitute, or if they were coerced, threatened and taken advantage of.

Coming from a life of abuse and entrapment in the sex industry, I can honestly say that no one wants to be a prostitute, stripper or porn star. No one grows up fantasizing about having men do unthinkable things to them for money. Anyone who ends up on the streets has had some type of pain in their life. They all need to be recovered, and then given the tools required to start the journey into healing. They all need love. Too many times well-meaning Christians would show up at the bikini club I was working at and yell horrible hate-filled things at us, holding signs and telling us we were going to hell. That is also not the way to help. We must always approach this subject and those affected by it with love and understanding.

There are many different ways someone can end up in a brothel, strip club, or on the streets. To truly make a difference in these victims lives we must understand with that life comes trauma and pain. The trauma stays long after they have escaped those situations. I share these stories with you so you can understand how these precious lives are affected by the world of sexual abuse. To identify, help and recover these precious souls, I feel you also need to understand the emotional war that is going on inside of them.

Sex trafficked victims can also be found in massage parlors, steam rooms, gentlemen clubs, call girls and similar establishments. Many of these so-called sex workers are not there because they want to be. Escorts—as in those who are highly paid to go on dates—can also be victims of sex trafficking. If you come across someone you believe is in trouble, please call the hotline. One call could save a life.

Many of these victims are being controlled by pimps. There are a few different types of pimps that entrap girls and boys in sex trafficking. The terms used to describe them are Gorilla, Romeo and Daddy. A Gorilla or Guerilla pimp uses physical violence to control his victims. A Romeo—or sometimes referred to as a finesse pimp—uses psychological abuse and manipulation through a false relationship. A Daddy pimp will provide for the victim, creating a false identify of protection and love. These different types of pimps entrap their victims using different techniques, but all of them use physical violence and manipulation to get the victim to start working for them.

Guerrilla Pimp

Guerrilla traffickers use what's called "Guerrilla pimping" to keep the girls enslaved. They use violence and drugs to prevent them from escaping and to make sure they keep performing. Many drug cartels have gone from selling a drug that they can only sell once, to enslaving girls and selling them over and over again. An organization called GEMS has many horror stories of survivors they have rescued. These girls have had their vaginas sliced with box cutters, their fingernails plucked out, beaten with belts, chains, rods and so many more unthinkable things. Pimps use destructive methods to keep the girls in fear and force them to have sex with 20-50 men a night. The stats for the starting age of girls entering prostitution keeps changing and is currently being disputed. Most say 12-14 years old—although another study says 19. There are many children that are abused from birth, being groomed for human trafficking. What is average anyway? None of this is average.

The fact that there are 4, 8, and 11-year-old girls trapped in sex trafficking is enraging.

It's becoming more and more common for the traffickers to bring the "product" to where the clients are. That's why we are seeing an increase in sex trafficking in America. Certain events spike the demand for prostitutes. The Super Bowl is the largest sex trafficking breeding ground in America. It's devastating to think about a 13-year-old girl who should be going to middle school, painting her nails and talking on the phone to her friends is instead being held in the back of a van at the Super Bowl as men rape her over and over again. She can hear the cheers in the background, and no one can hear her cries.

The Romeo, Finesse or Boyfriend pimp

Everyone desires to be loved and seen. Consider a girl who is having problems at home, a college girl who feels undesirable and unwanted, a latchkey kid who comes home to an empty house, or the woman who feels she has no one to talk to and is starving for attention. Enter, the perfect guy, he listens and gives her ample attention. He hears her hardships and offers a shoulder to cry on. Slowly this "boyfriend" begins to gain her trust. Next, he starts to shower her in gifts. Buying her new clothes, taking her out to nice restaurants, and giving her jewelry. She feels as if she has finally found someone who truly cares for her and desires the best for her. Then one day, there is a fight at her home. Dad's drunk again, her husband beats her, or an eviction notice comes in the mail. The breaking point arrives, and she is devastated. For many at risk, it's just everyday life that has them on the brink of wanting to run and get away from it all. The boyfriend is once again there and listening, and then offers a solution. "Let's just ran away together."

They make plans to meet and drive away into the sunset. The girl is filled with the promise of adventure and a new life waiting for her. That is, until they make it across state lines, and she is sold to the traffickers her "boyfriend" has been working with. She is traded like a used car, never to be heard from again. If she was an adult, it would just look like she got tired and left. As a teenager, it's assumed she ran away. What these girls don't know is that their so-called boyfriends were working on a few girls at a time, posing as the perfect guy, just waiting for when life disappoints so that he can swoop in with all the answers.

When I was speaking at inner-city schools, these types of stories were the best ones to focus on. It's surprising how many girls would come up to me afterward and say that their friend is in trouble. They just knew something was off about their friend's boyfriend. The person who is being deceived usually knows something is off, but their desperation for love or acceptance overrides that gut feeling. They want so badly for this incredible love of their life to be real. Don't dismiss how dangerous desiring acceptance can be. It's in our inner being to want to be loved, feel beautiful or handsome, and desirable.

Kindness to those we bypass daily can go a very long way. A smile, hug, or a kind gesture nourishes the soul and creates powerful change and beauty in this world.

Daddy Pimp

The perfect example of a Daddy pimp is what is happening with the women in prison. For women who are incarcerated, there is another danger waiting for them when they are released. Found in public records are these women's names and why they were incarcerated. Predators are searching for this information and especially for anyone who is in prison on prostitution charges. It's becomes a horrible cycle for these women. Many survivors end up in prison on charges for crimes they were forced to do. They never wanted to be in that situation to begin with, and now, instead of being helped by the system, they are being punished. It's heartbreaking to think about being forced by a family member, someone you trusted, or a stranger to sell your body for sex and then be put in prison by the very system you were hoping would have provided justice.

In prison, these survivors are left with psychological scars and deep feelings of abandonment, leaving them vulnerable victimization. Predators then proceed to write these women and befriend them, sending them money for their accounts and supporting them emotionally. In the letters, they promise a better life when they get out, offering for the girl to come live with them. Many women who have been incarcerated are very lonely. Their families and friends have abandoned them after being placed in prison. To have someone who seems to care write to them and give them money is a dream come true. They latch onto the mysterious pen pal, hoping that someone still wants them and cares for them. Finding a job on the outs is almost impossible since they have to declare why they were in prison to their new employer.

Can we think about this for a second? Imagine having to declare that you are a prostitute to every employer? Eventually, all of your co-workers will find out. The way people judge and treat those who have been sexually exploited is unbelievable. Men take advantage of their position of power and expect that they would want to give sexual favors on the job. Co-workers call names like "slut" or "whore." Other women don't trust them around their men. A stigma is placed on those coming out of the sex industry. How can one truly turn their life around when everyone around them expects them to be a certain way?

On the day of being released, it is mandatory in some states, that someone is there to pick them up. Since their friends and family are no longer in contact with them, they turn to the only person who has been there for them. Their new "daddy" is there to pick them up—sometimes with new clothes, booze and money to shower them with. After seeming to be the perfect provider and lover, things begin to change for the worse. The pimp starts demanding they pay him back for everything that he has done for them, so he forces them into working for him.

There was a case of a man in Florida who was working on over twenty girls at a time. Once they moved in with him, they were not allowed to leave. He forced them to pay him back through prostitution. He was convicted and caught because someone called in a tip.

Runaways

When a child runs away, the statistics are alarming, and time is not on their side. Although the numbers keep changing and the statistics are not exact, the majority of organizations report that within 48 hours, 70% of runaway teens will become victims of human trafficking. They could be approached by a pimp, trucker or just about any other person wanting to exploit them. Many runaways resort to survival sex, where they exchange sex for food or a place to stay. Many get taken and enslaved in sex trafficking where they are beaten and raped. Many are drugged immediately with heroin or another drug that has painful withdrawal. Some are left for dead on the streets or abandoned half-alive. When police officers find them, they are taken to jail and assumed to be a prostitute. Once they are released, the trafficker or pimp is there waiting for them.

There are gut-wrenching testimonies of many young runaways. I have watched video after video of moms who would not give up looking for their daughters, many of whom were found on the dark web being sold for sex. It's painful to watch the mothers break down crying and screaming, "no, not my daughter." I feel most parents hold their breath hoping their child will just be found in an overnight diner, sitting in a back booth mad at the world. Many of these mothers have been able to rescue their children using the help of numerous resources, such as a human trafficking task force, private detectives, and government task forces run by the police, FBI or ICE.

There is another at-risk group that I feel I should mention. The group acronym changes as more and more people groups are identified and added in. The LGBTQ+ (Lesbian, Gay, Bisexual, Transgender, Genderqueer) community are significant targets for traffickers. After confronting their caregivers about their sexual identity, they are kicked out of their homes, ignored, or bullied. They feel unwanted and separated from society. A high number go to the internet for acceptance and answers about their sexuality. That makes this group of teens at risk for online predators. If this is something you are passionate about, there are many groups out there that focus just on this group of kids.

In many states, running away is a criminal act. Parents are responsible for keeping their children in their home until they are eighteen years old. Children run away from an abusive situation or unsafe environment only to find themselves in worse conditions on the streets. They are afraid of going to the authorities about what is happening in fear of going to jail or back to their unsafe home. It makes it difficult to connect with these kids and get them the help they need. Volunteering at shelters that help runaway teens would be a great way of fighting on the front lines and making an impact in a child's life.

Truckers

The trucking industry has been used for the selling, soliciting, exploiting, transporting and harboring of victims for many years. Many truckers come across traffickers and their victims daily and are unaware of the indicators, so they go about their normal routine. They may come across someone transporting a shipment of slaves, or another trucker pimping out a runaway in the back of his truck. Many truckers come across someone who is in danger and never know it.

Over the decades, traffickers are continually changing the ways they use the trucking industry. In the 70's, if a trucker had a girl he pimped out of the back of his truck, he would just tell everyone. He would go up and knock on the doors of truckers' and tell them they could pay for sex. In the early 2000's, they would announce they have a lizard—aka, a sex slave—coming in hot.

Organizations like Truckers Against Trafficking have made a considerable impact on combating human trafficking within the trucking industry. When they first started their organization, I would help them by putting posters up at every truck stop. I kept a big stack in my car, and every time I went to fill up, I would ask if I could put a poster up. A simple act of raising awareness has made a significant impact. Many truckers were unaware of what human trafficking was, and even if they did see something that looked questionable, they had no idea what to do about it. By teaching truckers what to look out for, lives are being saved. In the state of Colorado, a law has been implemented that in order to get your trucking license, you must attend a human trafficking awareness course. There are many hope-filled stories from truckers who have called the hotline with the information given and lives saved. Many truckers want to do good and make a difference, they just need to be empowered, educated and given the right tools to do so.

Sleepovers

This one will make any parent second guess where their child is. My goal is not to instill fear into you as a parent, but I do want you to be aware of the dangers out there. If it's not human trafficking, it could be sexual abuse. There are too many stories of children being sexually abused during sleepovers. I have a personal story that happened to me in elementary school, and many have shared their stories with me.

I've also had the privilege of knowing a few child sex crime police officers, and they shared too many stories that any one person should have never encountered. One detective was our neighbor, and he had a strict no sleepover rule. I always thought it was odd until I started to learn more about what type of things go on during sleepovers. It's not usually the parents who are the abusers. It's the older siblings, house guests, or relatives. There are even cases of children saying they are at someone's house, but instead are being pimped out on the streets.

Under the cases of human trafficking, it is much more of a detailed system of lies and threats. First, the trafficker will identify their next victim. They may approach them after school or when they are alone. They have collected information on their victim's family and loved ones. They threaten the child that if they do not lie about sleeping over at a friend's house, bad things will happen to the ones they love. They make threats against their victim's family, promising to kill their little sister, mom or dad if they don't do what they say. The child does as the trafficker demands and meets with them in secret. They are then sold for sex all weekend long, allowed to leave and go back home Sunday night.

Please look for signs that your child may be a victim. Have they changed in attitude? Lost their appetite? Started to wear long sleeves in summer? Lost or gained weight? Seem depressed, withdrawn or anxious? They could have new tattoos or branding, suddenly own expensive new clothes or come home with manicures and pedicures. These are just a few signs your child could be a victim of sexual exploitation.

As a parent, I encourage you to have open conversations about what's allowed to be touched on your child's body. A great way of doing this with younger children is using a bathing suit as an example. Whatever their bathing suit covers should never be touched by anyone, and if it is, they need to tell you immediately. As your child gets older, these conversations may be more embarrassing and uncomfortable to have. Having raised three boys, I consider it a good day if I've offended my child in some way with my over-parenting skills.

I have been known to be overzealous at times when it comes to tackling the tough questions at the worst times. For instance, there might have once been a question asked about drugs at my kids' school. The principle may have been interrogated by someone's mom about what he was doing about said problem. My children may have gotten multiple texts about some crazy lady asking about drugs at the back-to-school night. And they could have possibly found out that the crazy lady was their mom. . .

Of course, this has neither been confirmed nor denied.

You don't have to go that far, but please call and speak with the other parents or caregivers to make sure they will be home the whole night of the sleepover. Ask about their rules around alcohol and curfew. Establishing rules with your children ahead of time about meeting the parents first helps dissolve arguments later. Remember that knowledge is power. Trust me, it's easier to implement the rules early on. If your children are older, it may require a conversation and being very open with them about why you are paying closer attention to their whereabouts.

This next story brings out the mamma bear in me. It's a true story about a girl around the age of seventeen who lived in a wealthy area on the East Coast and has loving parents. She went to an excellent high school and lived a normal teenager life. Her future was filled with hopes, dreams, and college acceptance letters. One night she went to a party, and two boys there roofied her drink. They then took her to a back room and filmed themselves raping her. The next day they blackmailed her with the tape. In fear of the boys' threats and the shame she would bare if the video made it to social media, this scared, precious girl did what they asked of her. She would tell her parents she was sleeping over at a friend's house for the weekend, and then sneak out to meet the boys. They would then pimp her out to paying customers.

Eventually, the boys disappeared with her. When her parents found and rescued her, she didn't look like the seventeen-year-old daughter they had lost. The traffickers had given her breast implants, lip injections, and hair extensions. After being rescued, she never was the same again. The psychological abuse was too much, and she ended up dropping out of school and moving to Vegas working as a dancer.

Survivors many times will start to believe that they are worth only as much as people will pay for them. Girls will run back to that life because they cannot adjust to normal society. Staying drugged and accepting their destiny can be more comfortable than being sober and trying to rise above and deal with the psychological trauma.

I need you to remember this story. I need you to understand how these things are at play. It's not just at-risk kids living in the projects who become victims. Throw out any stereotypes that may be running through your mind. Anyone can be a victim. You may run into a girl like her. A girl that looks like she is trying to look way older than she really is. A girl that just doesn't seem to belong. There are things you can do to save girls like her.

Social Media

Social Media, video games, smartphones, chat rooms, forums or anything with access to the internet can be used as a tool for traffickers to find their next victim. They scroll and troll, looking for those who are vulnerable. And it's not just the girls we have to be concerned about; young boys can be victims too.

When teens post pictures that are exposing too much skin, pics of self-harm, or angry words about how they feel alone in the world, they become targets for predators. A girl showing a little bra and a sexy model face she learned from her favorite influencer on social media is a perfect example of the types of behavior predators look for. That picture tells them that she is looking for affirmation and wanting someone to notice her. The predators pose as a young boy interested in her and spark up a DM (Direct Message).

A little scientific fact: Teenagers and adults actually get a dopamine dose every time they post and someone responds with a positive comment. More and more teens are doing unthinkable things online just looking for validation.

As parents, we need to try to track and monitor our children's online activity. There are apps out there that help parents watch their children's online activity. Unfortunately, there are also ghost apps that help kids hide what they are really up to. A ghost app could look like a calculator but when you type in an equation, it brings you to a dark website. Some give parents fake accounts to follow while posting the real stuff under a different name or hidden account. Predators are getting smart at following their next victims on social media. Once they've identified who it is, it doesn't take too much effort to find and track them. It's as simple as watching where they check in, sending a DM asking to meet, and watching for what events they are going to. With some smooth talk, a flashy smile and a believable story, they coerce the teen to come with them.

Other times the trafficker will pose as a friend in an online chat room or video game and suggest they meet up. They make fake social media accounts and pose as a young girl to friend another girl, when actually they are a 40-year-old male predator. The term for this is "Catfish." There are many ways for someone to be tricked and then taken. We must train our youth how to protect themselves. Explaining to your children that they need to notify you if someone you don't know sends them a DM and wants to meet. Have open conversations around your rules for social media and expectations on how your child should behave and present themselves.

A good rule to have is to never meet someone for the first time without having someone with you and making it at a very public place. When parking your car, ensure that it's under a street light. Don't park next to sketchy vans. If you get a check or a bad feeling, listen to those feelings. Even adults need to be careful.

Online dating is all the rage, and really, from what I've seen, it is also the main way people are meeting nowadays. Online dating is here to stay. I really enjoy meeting new friends from Facebook in person. There are safe ways to meet your new friends without jeopardizing your safety. I encourage you to use one of the many free apps out there that allow you to do a video call first. This way you will know the person is who they say they are. After you have acknowledged that they are the person in the picture and are comfortable with them. Then you can meet them in person at a public place, driving separately so you can leave at any time if you feel uncomfortable. Let a friend know where you will be on your date or meet up and give them the name of the person you're meeting. There is a whole show called Catfish where people meet their online friends for the first time. They believe they have fallen in love with one person, but it's never the person they thought. This show is so scary to me because it proves that so many people out there trust a profile picture and talk to complete strangers without knowing who they really are while developing a relationship with them.

Traveling

When the Liam Neeson movie, Taken, first came out, I was astonished at how accurate it was. It displayed how most girls that are taken are immediately drugged and sold into sex trafficking. It displayed the mistakes young girls can make when traveling by giving away too much information. It also exposed the dark world of auctioning off virgins.

When traveling, you must be on high alert—especially college-aged girls traveling in small groups or by themselves. There are a few tactics that traffickers use to entrap travelers. Some of those tactics include: accidental run-ins and meet-ups at airports, bus stops, even shopping malls are common breading grounds for predators.

Once the trafficker as identified their prey that begin using social engineering tactics to gather information. They are hoping to find out where you are staying, if you are alone, how long you will be there and why you are traveling. Using this information, they can track their next victim down and exploit them. It's imperative that as a traveler you never give that kind of information out to a stranger or post it on social media. Spoiler alert: in the movie, the girls told the young trafficker that they were alone and where they were staying. The men came in and took the girls, and like too many cases, the girls were abused and enslaved in sex trafficking. The non-virgin friend was drugged, beaten and raped. She was then forced to be a sex slave. The daughter of Liam Neeson was a virgin and very true to fact, virgins go for more money. She was taken to an auction were her virginity would be sold to the highest bidder. These types of sales happen online every day.

When posting on social media, never check in or tell what city you will be in at the very moment you are there. I know lots of you like to blog. It's okay if you check in after you have left. No one will know it was the day before. Don't post your travel itinerary online. If you are a US citizen traveling outside of the country, please check in with the US Embassy in the country you are visiting. If something were to happen, the Embassy now has the power to assist in rescuing you. It's also a great idea in case of a natural disaster or war breaking out to know if they should look for you.

Familial Trafficking

There are cases of relatives trafficking their family members. Instances where a single mom who has to work, has a relative offer to watch their child for free, and while the mother is away, the child is pimped out. The child is raped over and over and then threatened to keep silent or their mother will die. Sometimes it's the parent that is selling their child for sex. There was a mother who was caught and convicted of selling her special needs daughter for sex. Some are powerful families that have ties to gangs and pimps. Others use the abuse for power and control. Using tactics like gas lighting, where the victim starts to question their thoughts and reality. Children who are being trafficked usually have been sexually abused since birth. They grow up thinking that violence and rape are normal. They don't understand that this is not the way families behave. This is also the most underreported type of trafficking, because the children will not report a family member.

I'm so grateful for mandatory reporting and the hotline numbers. Some teachers and doctors used to not speak up in fear of losing their jobs. Now there are many tools for anyone to use to report without risk to themselves. I've been asked before if I'm scared of speaking up. Some say that I'm at risk of being harmed because of my outspokenness. It never dawned on me to be fearful of such a thing. If someone is in need, I have never thought twice about answering the call. But I'm glad I get asked this question. It reminds me that there are people who are fearful of speaking up or getting involved. By bringing you this information and the tools to get involved I truly hope that all fears of speaking up are put to rest, and that you feel confident and capable of knowing what to do if you come into contact with a victim.

Foster Care and Adoption

The foster care system is a beautiful program in place for children waiting for a forever home. I encourage you that being a foster parent is a great way to make an impact and change lives. We need more caring individuals to love these hurting children. Unfortunately, there have been cases of foster care guardians pimping out children, using them for forced labor and sexual exploitation.

The adoption process is blessing to many couples and individuals. It's a way for orphaned children to find forever families. But there are people out there who are taking advantage of the fact that someone is willing to pay for a child. They kidnap kids from their families and then say they are orphans. When adopting, do your due diligence and make sure the agency has a good record and follows the laws.

International Students

There have also been cases of people exploiting international students. They send the child to school and then at night, pimp the child out. Some use the international student for slave labor, forcing them to act as unpaid housekeepers.

I will go over indicators that will help you identify victims. If you are a teacher, social worker, or school volunteer, knowing these indicators can save lives. The case with the international students was exposed by someone who knew what to look for. The children would go to school and never leave their house once they came home. The neighbors never saw them out playing or at after-school events. Someone got a check in their gut and reported it. Making a difference is just that simple.

This chapter was focused on sex trafficking in America, but don't forget that all types of human trafficking are in America. Any kind of slavery is wrong and needs to be eradicated. There are homes, factories, businesses, farms and more in America that are willfully violating human rights by forcing slave labor.

I can't wait to hear all your testimonies on what you have done to fight human trafficking. Together we can make a difference. Together we are strong, and a mighty force to be reckoned with. Let's answer the call to arms against human trafficking and take back our neighborhoods, cities, states, and country.

NOTES

NOTES

IN A GENTLE WAY,
YOU CAN SHAKE THE WORLD
- GANDHI

4 CHAPTER FOUR
Answering the Call

From sex trafficking to labor trafficking and everything in between there is a place for you in this fight. Understanding the different types of human trafficking has opened my eyes. I can no longer look at a discount clothing store that makes mass-produced clothing and not wonder how many slaves it took to make that outfit. After watching The Dark Side of Chocolate—a movie about child slavery—I refuse to eat a chocolate bar that's not registered fair trade. I'd rather pay a little more for someone to have a better life. I may eat less of it, but at least I'm not supporting inhumane business practices. The same is true with bananas, coffee, cotton, shrimp, sugar and tea. All these products are known for violating human rights laws so that they can offer the products at a lower price. I do my best, but I most likely still own a cotton shirt that used slave labor, and I really hope my diamond ring was created ethically. I slip up and go to the mall when I know there are online stores I could go shop at with a cause. I am aware and when possible, I do what I can with the knowledge I have. You don't have to go nuts about it and yell at your friends who are eating cheap chocolate. Just be aware and be a socially responsible consumer.

Now that you are becoming aware, you may also notice these things popping up in your life. Even watching certain shows and movies seemed okay until your eyes have been opened to this world. Movies like, Pretty Woman continue to sadden me, and questions still flood my mind. How many young girls are trapped in that life and end up like their friend Marie? Dead in a dumpster after a pimp has used them and beaten the life out of them? The sad reality is that most women trapped in that life end up just like Marie.

I grew up listening to Reba McEntire singing about "Fancy" and how her mother said, "here's your one chance, Fancy, don't let me down, just be nice to the gentlemen, Fancy, and they'll be nice to you." Nope. Can't listen to it without crying and my heart breaking for the real-life cases of mothers who have turned out their daughters. Don't get me started on video games like Grand Theft Auto. This especially gets to me and pushes my abolitionist buttons. How can someone sit there and think beating up a prostitute is entertainment? In the game, you can request sexual favors, and she will scream in delight for you, after that, you're encouraged to run her over and beat her to death to get your money back. I can't help but wonder what is wrong with the world. Sometimes, I worry that I may give up on mankind altogether.

But focusing on the pain, hurt and wrong doings of evil people will not help. It will just make us into cynical, angry people. We must hold onto the belief that love conquers all. The real question is one that I'm hoping we can answer together: when there are so many evil people and so much pain in this world, what can be done to stop it?

There is so much hope, so much joy, and so much action that can be done that I could fill a book with it (oh, wait, that's exactly what I am doing). Many don't know what to do and get so frustrated when looking to fight human trafficking that they just start their own non-profit or do nothing at all. I know of families who sold everything they have and move to a foreign country to help these slaves, which is impressive and takes guts.

Let's face it, most of us have no desire to have that level of commitment. There is nothing wrong with saying, "I want to do something, just not change my whole life and give up all I have." Other well-meaning individuals have been so angered by what they have seen and learned that they start volunteering like it's a second job. But these people often get overwhelmed with all that needs to be done, and the lack of incoming funds, and the red tape of the non-profit world quickly burns them out.

I've seen organizations come and go. I've also seen organizations fighting over money and who is doing what. I've seen the ugly side of fighting human trafficking. Some organizations want you to have a degree and raise funds for your salary. Others prefer for you to donate and give money as your way of getting involved. One of my desires for this book is to be a guide for an organization to help their volunteers give and get involved. I know many organizations are overwhelmed by the task at hand that they don't know how to plug-in eager individuals raising their hands saying, "Put me in, coach." I've been keeping track of organizations that are fighting human trafficking, and the list grows each day. I have people come up to me and ask if I've heard of this organization or that one. There are plenty of organizations that have joined in on the fight. And yes, giving makes a difference. Starting an organization can create change—many have and will continue to do so.

The main reason I'm writing this book is for the rest of us. Those who want to do more than just give money, but not as much as running a non-profit. Those of us who are SAHM's (stay-at-home-mom), working parents, DINKS (double-income-no-kids), entrepreneurs, doctors, lawyers, realtors, construction workers, or a local barista. Those of us who have incredibly demanding lives and don't need one more thing on our to-do list. Each day we wake up, hustle hard and enjoy life, working hard for our summer vacations and promotions. Life is good for many of us, and it's nice to walk in the sun and be grateful for all we have. We also have our own struggles which are sometimes overwhelming and life-changing. Some of our problems may be champagne problems; nevertheless, they are our problems and are significant to us. We are not being held as sex slaves or trapped in a trailer somewhere, but we do have car problems, demanding jobs, companies to run, and children who don't listen. We have stuff that we are going through.

Yet, you are not heartless or uncaring. You are aware that there is a problem out there and you want to do something, something more than just writing a check and not as much as starting another anti-human trafficking non-profit.

Now what?

How can you answer the call to arms against human trafficking?

I'm so thrilled you asked!

Here are a few practical ways you can make an impact. Some are easy, and some are a little bit harder. It doesn't matter if you do just the first one or none of them. The fact that you are reading this sentence means a difference has already been made. It's inevitable that you will tell at least one person, and that one person another, and the light will spread.

An impact will be made!

In the back of this book is a list for you with many different ways you can make an impact, and an action guide for you to fill out. It will help you develop a plan on how you can be the change this world needs, then implement that plan and make it happen. Small steps towards making a significant impact.

Get your pen and highlighter ready; it's time to take notes.

Highlight things you know you can do, anything that jumps out on the page to you.

Take notes of ideas that come up as you read through these.

Write all over this book!

When you get to the action guide, you can refer to your notes and ideas.

Let's dive into the top ten things you can do to make an impact today.

TOP 10 Ways to Make a Difference

#1 Save the Hotline number in your phone

If there is only ONE thing you do, it should be this: put the Hotline number in your phone. The hotline is currently run by Polaris and you can find more info about them by visiting their website. https://humantraffickinghotline.org

Take out your phone right now and program this number into it:

Call: 1-888-373-7888
Text: 233733 (Text "HELP" or "INFO") 24 hrs, 7 days a week

If you see anything at all or have questions, give them a call. Share this number with everyone you know, on social media, at work, church, everywhere. Lives could be saved, a daughter rescued, hope restored. If you're a realtor, teacher, doctor, nurse, flight attendant, trucker, a worker at an airport or bus stop, please pay attention.

Chances are that victims are coming in and out of your places of work. Just search your profession or talents and human trafficking on the internet.

(In the search engine, type: the name of your profession + human trafficking)

You will see lots of information come up about how you can spot a victim. For everyone else who shops at the mall, travels, goes to sporting events, a night out, or leaves their house for any reason, be on alert as well.

There are also local numbers for your area. You can search online for the human trafficking hotline number in your city.

Extra credit time! Find out who in your local police department is in charge of human trafficking cases. Ask them who you should call if you know you've come across a victim. Ask them lots of questions and learn what it looks like in your area.

Go ahead. Put the book down for a second and put that number in your phone. 1-888-373-7888

#2 Learn the indicators of human trafficking

Congratulations, you have saved the hotline number in your phone! You have done something to stop human trafficking.

Now what? For you to be an aware citizen and be able to prevent human trafficking, you must be able to identify possible trafficking situations. The next step is to learn the indicators of human trafficking.

Below is a list of things to be aware of and to look out for. If you feel you have come across a possible human trafficking situation, call the hotline right away. If you know you have come across a victim, call the police.

Some things to look for would be:

Does your neighbor have cars coming in out of their home all day long? I'm not talking about your neighbor who is in direct sales and is having another party—although, if you feel something is weird is going on with them, go ahead and call. It's better to be safe and wrong than to find out you could have saved a life but didn't.

Do you know someone who has a maid who never leaves the house and may be sleeping in the garage? A young girl that is with a gentleman much older than her who does not appear to be a relative?

When you visit a place, is there higher than usual security systems in place? Do you see security cameras everywhere? Bars covering their windows with dark curtains. Employees that rarely leave their workplace. How about businesses that only service male clients?

Have you ever met someone you thought may be in trouble? A door-to-door magazine salesperson, a girl at the truck stop, nail salon, or massage parlor?

A victim could be a child you met at a fast food restaurant, in your classroom, or a roadside vendor. Below is a comprehensive list for teachers, doctors, nurses, flight attendants, truckers and the like to learn and memorize. There are also classes you can take to learn more. If you are in one of these professions, I highly recommend you look up a class near you.

Here are a few signs to look out for that might indicate someone is in trouble:

- Seem fearful

- Not allowed to talk for themselves

- No passport or mention that someone else has their documentation

- Show signs of psychological abuse, seem distant or hopeless

- Have bruises that they hide

- Talk about having to pay off debts

- Get paid less than minimum wage

- Seem extremely tired or sleep in odd places

- Are not free to come and go as they please

- Are under 18-years-old in commercial sex

- Mention that their job was not what they were hired for

- Seem to be poorly taken care of—medically and physically

- Lack their own money and have no financial records or belongings

- Mention that they are just visiting but will not tell you where they are from or going.

- Seem not to know what the date or time is

- When speaking with them, they seem to have a very inconsistent storyline

- Move a lot and don't stay in one place too long

- Talk or speech seems scripted, as if someone has told them what to say

- Show signs of branding. It could be tattoos or burn marks

- Lie about their age

- Have to ask permission to do the most basic things such as use the bathroom, sleep, eat, etc.

- Are in a relationship with a very dominating individual

- Afraid of law enforcement or other people trying to help

- Avoid eye contact

- Are dressed inappropriately for the weather

- A child who seems uncomfortable when they sit down

- A child that acts quirky

- Display Stockholm Syndrome; they have misplaced loyalty to the trafficker

- Have decreased/disjointed memory

- Are unable to recall traumatic events accurately

- Memories are triggered by related sensory information: sight, sound, touch, etc.

Display PTSD symptoms such as:

- Intrusive recall flashbacks

- Intense psychological distress (anger or anxiety) when exposed to reminders of the trauma

- Nightmares; sleep disturbance; insomnia

- Detachment; isolation; estrangement

- Depression

- Numbing; lack of effect

- Anger or irritability

- Aggression

- Exaggerated, startled responses

- Impulsiveness

- Hyper vigilance

Let's break it down some more and categorize what you may see in victims within the different types of human trafficking. I want to thank the Human Trafficking Survivor Coalition (HTSC) for helping me create a more comprehensive list. I spoke with one survivor, Kelly Dore, who also runs the HTSC and she said that teachers and doctors had an opportunity to reach out to her but never did. She was repeatedly sexually abused at home. There were signs and indicators she showed. Knowing these indicators can save a life, please don't dismiss them.

If you would like to learn more and dig deeper into identifying child survivors, research ACE (Adverse Childhood Experiences); it's an informative study on how abuse can manifest in a survivor's life. By knowing how abuse affects these precious children, you will be able to identify survivors more accurately.

If you are a teacher, social worker, youth pastor, or anything that brings you around children often, I urge you to go get as much training as you can on how to identify victims.

Health indicators of Labor Trafficking:

- Physical

- Musculoskeletal and ergonomic injuries

- Malnutrition/Dehydration

- Lack of routine screening and prevention of care

- Poor dental hygiene

- Untreated skin infections/inflammations

- Inflammations injuries or illness from exposure to harmful chemicals/unsafe water

- Eye issues or vision complaints

- Somatization—recurring medical conditions

Behavioral indicators of Labor Trafficking:

- Anxiety/ Panic attacks

- Stories don't line up or conflict with each other

- Paranoid behavior

- Can't make decisions; indecisive

- Irritability

Health indicators of Child Sex Trafficking:

- Pregnancy at a young age

- Reoccurring health issues

- Burn marks, bruises or cuts

- Evidence of abortions at a young age

- Early sexual initiation

- Trauma to the vagina/ rectum area

- Symptoms of sexually transmitted Infection and/or urinary tract infection
- An abnormal number of sexual partners for a young age

Behavioral indicators of Child Sex Trafficking:

- History of running away from home or foster care placements

- Skipping school or not going altogether

- Highly sexualized or indecent behavior and dressing

- Angry/aggressive with staff

- Depressed mood or no emotions at all

- Signs of drug or alcohol abuse

- Will not speak without an adult present

- Fearful

- Can't sit still and seems to be uncomfortable sitting down

It could be a place of business that catches your eye, a home that seems to have something else going on, a person that appears to be in distress, or it could be you. If you have any feeling or thought that someone could be in trouble, please do not hesitate to call the hotline. Don't worry, you can't get in trouble if it was a false call. It's always better to be safe than sorry. But maybe you were the third person that week to call about that house on the corner. The hotline will take that info to the local authorities to start building a case.

Remember my story about the mom that reached out to me about her runaway teenage daughter? I'm not going to lie, I was very overwhelmed. I thought to myself, "Who am I? I've been reading about this and talking about it, but who am I to be fighting it on this level?" Who was I? I was someone who cared and had the information necessary to help stop human trafficking.

#3 Educate Yourself

Now that you have the hotline number in your phone and you know some key things to watch for, it's time to dig deeper. It's time to start learning about what human trafficking looks like in your city. Each city is different, taking many shapes and forms. In every city, there are different cultures, agriculture, and demands.

In consideration of your talents and gifts, review the big list of ways to fight human trafficking in the back of this book, then start searching the internet to match your talents and gifts with human trafficking in your city. You will be surprised at how much information is out there when you start looking for it.

Begin reading books and watching movies on the areas that have made an impact on your heart. There is a multitude of information out there to find, research and devour. I encourage you to discover a few areas that you are passionate about.

Is it the sex trade? Labor? Organ harvesting? Child brides? Buying sustainable goods? Or it could be that you just want to keep your county, city, or even neighborhood safe.

Maybe your focus will be on keeping it out of your local schools, colleges, and businesses. Listen to your heart. Your passion will guide you and fuel you for this fight. Go and talk to your local firemen, police, and chamber of commerce. Learn what they know. If there is not a spokesperson for your area, you could volunteer to be that person. The more you know, the more power you take from the enemy and the harder it will be for traffickers to hide in plain sight.

I believe that knowledge is a light that we can shine in the dark places. Imagine everyone in your community knowing what to look for. Do you think that a house could continue to operate a sex trafficking ring on your block with the knowledge you now have?

The answer is no.

How about that one business that seems only to allow men and has high security? When aware citizens are continually asking questions, police are responding to tips from the trafficking hotline, and customers start asking the girls if they are being held against their will, the traffickers will have no other choice then to move their operation, or even better, shut it down.

I'm not naïve enough to say we can end human trafficking altogether—slavery has been around since the fall of man—but I do believe we can stand firm together and make it impossible to operate in our towns. We can prevent it from spreading by using education and empowerment as or weapon.

Be empowered, learn all you can and shine those lights so bright that the darkness must flee!

#4 Host a Bash Slavery party

Now that you have all this knowledge in your heart and mind, it's time to start sharing it. I am not suggesting you hop on a stage and talk to a thousand people you don't know. Take a few breaths and relax (unless that's your thing, then go for it). What I am hoping is that you will host a Bash Slavery party.

What is a Bash Slavery party?

It's a party with the focus of raising awareness around human trafficking. All you have to do is invite your friends and family over to your house, have some snacks and drinks, and then watch one of your favorite human trafficking movies or review a book. It can be a stand alone party or combined with a birthday, bunco game night or etc.

While you're at it, go ahead and share the hotline number and encourage your guests to save it in their phones— you can even share copies of this book. And if you're feeling extra ambitious, see if you can collect donations to give to your favorite organization fighting human trafficking.

The word "bash" can be used to mean two different things: to strike hard and violently, or to celebrate and throw a party.

Let's do both in one night. If you have a networking company and are throwing house parties to build your business, consider combining it with a Bash Slavery party.
Have information near the food about human trafficking. Donate a percentage of the sales to fight human trafficking. Maybe even give a 5-minute speech about why this movement is important to you.

I once attended an essential oils party, at the end of which, they played a movie called, The Abolitionists. The essential oil organization had just announced that they will be supporting Operation Underground Railroad. It was a great night of friends, oils, education, and laughter.

It also just so happened to be the night I decided to write this book. I'm not part of the direct sales company, but I do use the products. My friend invited me knowing my passion for fighting human trafficking. Everyone started asking me so many questions about how they can get involved. They wanted to know what action they could take. I started to think about all the speeches I've given, conferences I've attended and people I have shared this subject with. The number one question I get is, "how can I take action?" Hence, the birth of Battle Cry and a year-long journey in creating a book that answers that very question.

There are many different ways to throw a Bash Slavery party and use the knowledge you have to fight human trafficking. You can host a Super Bowl party, and then, before opening the keg, explain what human trafficking is and how the super bowl is the biggest night for sex trafficking.

You can have a Friday night BBQ and leave small chalkboard signs around with hotline numbers, statistics, and information to empower your friends to answer the call to arms against human trafficking. From your living room to coffee shops, there is never a wrong time to raise awareness! Well. . . I can think of one: don't use your toast at someone's wedding to explain child brides. That may not go over too well.

If you do throw a bash slavery party, please take a picture and share it on social media using #bashslavery. It will be fun to see how all of you are using parties to make a difference.

#5 Get Involved

The number one question I am asked is, "How do I get involved".

Many want to go overseas and rescue the girls out of brothels. I love this initiative, and if you're a trained fighter, please contact Operation Underground Railroad or a similar organization and offer your services. For those of us who only have six-packs and sniper skills in our dreams, there are many other ways to help out.

Research the organizations that are in your area and choose one to volunteer at. The action guide in this book will equipped you on how to do this. To be successful, you must focus on one thing at a time. If you try to do too many things you may get overwhelmed. Nowadays there are so many different ways to help that it could lead to analysis paralysis. There are tons of organization out there, and the choice may be hard. Let's approach this just like I do when I'm coaching in business. When you focus on one thing, you will be much more productive and effective in what you are doing. Completing the action guide in this book will also help you formulate a clear and attainable plan.

Now that you have found that one organization that you are going to support and be an advocate for, let's get you into the trenches.

Do they have a local chapter? If not, start one. If they do, join and attend the monthly meetings. Many have yearly fundraisers that they desperately need help with. Learn about the organization and then volunteer to be an advocate for them. Contact schools and local organizations and spread the word about what they are doing to combat human trafficking. Don't forget to hold a Bash Slavery party to raise funds and help financially support your favorite organization.

If running or joining a local chapter sounds too complicated, there are many other ways to get involved. Think about starting a book club. This would be a fun way to fight human trafficking with friends, over adult beverages, coffee or tea. Start a blog and collect articles about human trafficking, review movies and books and advertise local conferences. Make sure you look at the list at the end of this book for many more ideas.

Keep it simple, choose one thing that fits your talents, and then put it on your schedule. Plan a time to implement what you can commit to without feeling stressed. It's as easy as 1-2-3. Boom! You've saved the world!

Okay, maybe you haven't saved it, but the world is certainly a better place because you and your love.

#6 Shop Wisely

This is one of my favorite things to do: shop! Now you can have a great reason to go buy a new purse or gift for that special someone. Start with searching the web for your slave footprint and find out how many slaves it took for you to live your life—It's very eye-opening. Be an educated consumer and purchase sustainable goods. Find out which companies you should avoid and which ones you should flock to. I'm trying to keep this book pretty relevant. Since apps and companies come and go, I won't say which ones to use. I'm sure there will be a significant number of resources for you. All you have to do is search "fair-trade app" and one should pop up.

Now that you are aware of where not to go shopping, it's time to find some fun places to shop. A few direct marketing companies are popping up with fair-trade practices, and many rescue centers tend to create and sell products made by survivors.

If you plan your shopping ahead of time, you will have some great gifts with beautiful stories to give. I really enjoy unique items from around the world with stories to tell. It's so fun when someone walks up and compliments my earrings or scarf and I get to re-tell a survivor's story. I know you men work differently. Here is some dating advice for you single men: give a gift that makes a difference. Tell the girl where it came from and who it impacted. You'll get big bonus points for being a guy that cares about others. Just don't go overboard and get weird and yell at people who still buy generic chocolate or other items that are known for slave labor. Remember, we do what we can, educate others, and then empower through love. Criticism and hate have never won anyone over.

#7 Lobby Local Politicians

If you geek out over politics, this is a fun one for you. Find out who your local politicians are and retrieve their contact information. Some governors already have human trafficking task forces in place. If they don't, offer to create one.

Write to your local politicians and explain to them the severity of the human trafficking epidemic, send them a copy of this book, describe how this horror is affecting our communities. Ask them what they are doing to combat the problem and say you would like to see more movement on this issue.

Get on the legislative sign-up list and be active in voicing your opinions on harsher punishments for the traffickers and more laws protecting the survivors. Go into your local police office and talk to them about human trafficking; ask them what they are seeing and how you can help.

Get to know the mayor of your town and ask if they are aware of what is going on in their community. If the Mayor doesn't have an appointed liaison bringing them information on human trafficking, offer your services to them.

Go to your local chamber of commerce and ask them if they are aware of the problem at hand. There are many levels of government, and all of them need to understand what is happening in their areas.

#8 Don't Buy Sex

The demand is fueling the sex trafficking industry. Without a demand, there would be no reason to sell young girls for sex. Breaking free from sexual addiction is not easy and can be very embarrassing to talk about or admit. Some have been raised to believe that sex is a rite of passage for a young man's life. Many have had fathers who have purchased a prostitute for them at a young age to usher them into manhood. Many have never considered that those girls don't want to be there or the physiological effect sex has on another person.

The average client purchasing little girls for sex is an white American man around 40 years of age, with an income of 70K or higher. If this is you and you're just now realizing that you have a problem, there are places you can go to get help. Sex addiction is a real illness, and it is destroying marriages and families.

One in every six men have been sexually abused in their lifetime. It's a high chance that many of you reading this are relating in some way. Many who have been abused ended up in some type of bondage. Please find a sexual addiction rehab and get help. You are not alone, there is help for you.

Some men who have purchased a child for sex are very embarrassed and remorseful. They explain that they didn't realize what was happening. They just started liking them younger and younger. The same patterns occur with rough and BDSM (bondage, discipline, sadism, masochism) sex.

Sexual desire and fulfillment can become addicting and can fall under the umbrella of mental illness. Get help before it's too late. Don't be part of the problem. Be the solution. Give up your porn, sex parties, and bachelor escapades; find other things to occupy your time. It may seem harmless now. It may be what your accustomed to, what every young man experiences, but it does not have to be. When you go to strip clubs, look at porn, or participate in any similar kind of activity while you are married, it hurts your wife and your family. If you're not married, it creates habits and expectations that can destroy future relationships.

If there was not a demand for this type of product, there would be no need to sell it. In these cases, the product is our youth. Your daughter, niece, nephew, wife, mother, sister, or brother—even you. This is not something that is done in dark closets without harm to anyone. These behaviors affect everyone. Now that you are aware, you have a responsibility to own up to certain habits you may be doing to fuel this industry. This is the hardest part of this entire book for me to write. It could also be the hardest part for you to read. I'm not here to judge, only to love and say that you have the strength to change. This does not define you. You are not alone. Many struggle silently with their sexual addictions.

I'm so proud of the women in our culture coming out and saying #metoo. Raising their voices and expressing how we should be treated and sought after. Will the men rise up and start being an example to the next generation on how to treat women? Will one man rise up and admit this is an issue and that it is not okay? Who will take charge and protect the next generation from sexual assault? We need men, women, and children united, taking a stand. The statistics of sexual abuse are alarmingly high for everyone. We must create a cultural disruption to the way our society is overdosed on sex.

Change has to start somewhere.
Allow it to begin with you.

#9 Pray and Practice Gratitude

There are many great resources online to help guide you in prayer for those trapped in modern-day slavery. Pray for the victims, for the families, for the abusers. Join or create a monthly prayer group. Or, start a monthly prayer group. Pray for the organizations and volunteers. Pray for the demand to end. Pray for those trapped in debt bondage, commercial labor, and horrible working conditions to be set free. There is so much to pray for and so much pain that needs to be healed.

Practice gratitude daily. There is so much to be grateful for. Have a thankful heart and focus on the fact that every day a survivor is being recovered and renewed. Be thankful for lives changed and slaves set free. Live in gratitude that we have the power to make a difference. Focusing on the good in this world and the good coming out of this movement will keep you from becoming depressed, bitter, or angry.

A grateful heart is a magnet for miracles.

#10 Give

Just like we need to spend wisely, I beg of you to give wisely. Don't just give to anyone claiming they are fighting human trafficking. Demand transparency. Do research and see how many victims they are reaching, and how much of the funds are going towards fighting human trafficking. How are they handling aftercare and reintroducing the girls to society? Who is backing them? What is their agenda? Be wise when giving set aside a monthly amount and give freely.

Be cheerful givers. Your life will prosper.

You will reap what you sow.

What you put out there returns to you.

One moment in time. One small decision can lead to a tsunami of change and lasting impact. Together we can end modern-day slavery. We can set the captives free, save lives, and renew hope. It doesn't take much. You don't have to be famous, rich or saturated in power and influence. You just have to be you with what you have today. Beautiful, amazing you. The very same person who picked up this book because they cared and wondered if they could be the change. I'm so thrilled you did! I'm very grateful we connected. You are my hope for the future. A future where we join together in love and create a butterfly effect that ends suffering and brings freedom to the captives all over the world.

Quoting the famous William Wallace—". . . they may take our lives, but they may never take our FREEDOM!" This is the end of Mel Gibson's speech in Braveheart. That battle scene is what I envisioned this book to be. I'm William Wallace in Braveheart, after seeing so much death and injustice, asking you, a volunteer army, to go to battle for something bigger than all of us. To fight for FREEDOM!!!!

Will you answer the call with me?

NOTES

THOSE WHO ARE CRAZY ENOUGH TO THINK
THEY CAN CHANGE THE WORLD USUALLY DO
-STEVE JOBS

5 | ACTION GUIDE

ACTION GUIDE

Are you ready to create a butterfly effect?

Time to flap your wings of change and cause a tsunami!

The next part of this book is a guide to help you answer the call to arms by identifying what your passions and talents are. Then, using that information, we will dive into the different areas you can make an impact.

So many of us get caught up in the grind of our daily lives. We say we want to help and have great intentions of doing just that. Then life gets in the way. We are too busy or overwhelmed at where to start, and then the holidays are here. Before we know it, years have passed, and our good intentions are still sitting on a shelf unused. With a subject as devastating as this, some of us get so excited that we jump right in. We go from task to task, organization-to-organization, and give everything we have and then some. At the end of the year, we find ourselves burnt out and quit.

Getting involved in fighting human trafficking can be overwhelming and discouraging. I want to bridge the gap between analysis paralysis and being burnt out by helping you create a plan that you can stick to and implement without burning out.

As you go through this guide, be honest with yourself about what level you can commit to long term. Seasons change and so may your commitment levels. Start with the season you are in, with the funds and time you currently have. If things change—as they always do—come back to this guide and review it.

Be prepared to do some work. Give yourself at least an hour to go through this. I encourage you to do the whole thing. It will not only help you understand how you can fight human trafficking, it can also help with your life, work and relationships.

Passions, Strengths, and Personality

For some of you, this may be your first introduction to the concept of a personality test and strength finders. There are many books out there and online test for you to dive deeper into understanding who you are and what you have to offer the world. I have found while coaching others that when a person knows what they are good at, they shine brighter. When you understand who you are, everything you do starts to flow. Finding flow in your life is crucial to being happy and not becoming overwhelmed.

When asked to do things that are not in alignment with your personality or strengths, it is like punching a gaping hole in your energy levels. You start to find that you hate everything around you, no amount of caffeine can help, and all joy is sucked out.

It starts to affect every aspect of your life. Too many volunteers who desire to help get plugged in where there is an immediate need. If that spot is not in alignment with the volunteer's strengths and personality, it will take its toll on the organization and volunteer.

Being honest with yourself as you go through this guide is of the utmost importance. It's not who you want to be, it is who you are. The best thing you can do is be who you are. When I take the D.I.S.C personality test, I laugh every time. I desire to be organized. The Air Force created some forced habits of organization in me, and if you ask people who know me, they would say I'm systematic and organized. On my personality test, it's almost a non-existent trait. It's a forced and learned behavior. It does not come naturally to me. If I were asked to be in an environment where I was tasked with doing lots of paperwork, creating systems, and crunching numbers, I would quickly find myself depressed and hating life. It doesn't mean that I can't do those things—I'm actually really good at them—I just don't enjoy them, and it's not something that comes naturally to me. If asked to do them for a long time, my joy and energy would be depleted, and that would not be a desirable outcome for anyone. Since my top personality trait is outgoing and energetic, place me in front of a crowd, and I can talk for hours and enjoy every moment of it. I love and enjoy managing people and getting them excited about things.

Since most of you will be doing this in a volunteer position, what would you rather be doing: something you are naturally good at, or something that drains the life out of you?

Organizational leaders take note. Volunteers are the lifeblood of non-profits. Having volunteers operating in their natural flow creates joy, energy, and progress.

Get ready to learn what your strengths are and what personality you are best matched with. Quick note: If you have had abuse in your past and a parent forced you to be a certain way, your results for the D.I.S.C test may come out unclear. For example, some of you have been coerced to be more introverted by well-meaning parents or teachers. Your extrovert actions were punished and deemed as bad behavior. So, at a young age you were taught to hold everything in. Maybe this guide will bring healing to you. I permit you to be you. Not the person that you feel you "need" to be, the person you are. There's no time like the present to be who you were meant to be.

FREE TO BE YOU

Step 1: D.I.S.C Test

This part is easy. There are a million of these tests you can take for free online and it takes only a few minutes to fill out. There are many different personality tests out there, but I like D.I.S.C tests for this practice. It gives a good understanding of what your strengths are, what drives you, and how you will respond to challenges in life. Another test I implore you to take is a spiritual gifting test. You can find these and many more online for free. Later you will use the results and match your personality and strengths with a list of how to fight human trafficking.

Go online and find a free DISC test.

Circle or highlight your top two results.

D.I.S.C

D - Dominant: outgoing, task-oriented.

I - Inspiring: a people person,

  usually in large groups, outgoing.

S - Supportive: a people person one on one, reserved.

C - Cautious: task-oriented, organized, reserved.

(Circle the top two you are)

Write down something that you learned and didn't realize about yourself:

Step 2: EXTROVERT vs INTROVERT

Another way to understand where and how you would be best suited in fighting human trafficking is by understanding which type of person you are.

There are two different types of people that we observe in life: EXTROVERT + INTROVERT

When reviewing the areas you can fight human trafficking, keep these in mind. If you are an introvert, you may not want to choose public speaking. You may want to host a small group of friends at your house instead. Remember there are no wrong answers. One specific quality or trait is not better than the other. We all make up one body. If we were all extroverts, who would be there to listen to anyone? This is a time to be true to yourself and embrace your personality for all it is. Don't compare yourself to others, just embrace who you are.

Take a look at the list below and circle the one you think you are. Pay attention to the qualities of each personality.

Are you an Introvert?

- Reflective

- Reserved

- Comfortable alone

- Has a small group of close friends

- Thinks before starting activities

- Energized by time alone

- Processes thoughts internally

- Is a "thinker" (often over thinks)

Are you an Extrovert?

- Outgoing

- People person

- Comfortable in groups

- Has many friends and acquaintances

- Jumps quickly into activities

- Gets energized from being around others

- Thinks aloud

- Talker

Put a big star next to the personality trait you believe you resonate with most.

It's funny when you look at the differences in the personalities. Some of you may know which one you were right away.

I enjoy taking these tests. I feel the more honest I can be with myself, the more authentic I become. I know, you were not expecting to do something like this when you picked up a book about human trafficking, just keep an open mind.

When you have completed this action guide, you will know more about yourself, your giftings and how you can change the world without adding additional stress to your life. I'm sure most of us have enough stress already. We don't need to be volunteering and find ourselves more stressed than before. Helping others should be enjoyable and rewarding.

By discovering your talents and identifying your personality, you will be an equipped warrior. You are a warrior, commissioned to set the captives free. It's empowering to say these declarations out loud:

I have been born for such a time as this

I have been anointed to proclaim freedom and set the captives free!

Step 3: Discovering your talents and gifts

Answer each question the best you can. The more honest you are with yourself the better. I believe we like to think of ourselves one way, but we often are a completely different person. We feel guilty about who we are, insecure, and self-conscious.

Why is that?

Maybe there was an adult figure that didn't like your natural qualities and was always pushing for you to be different. Maybe you've watched too many teen dramas, and it's shaped your opinion on how you should be. There are so many influences telling us we need to change or to be different than who we are, it can be overwhelming. Friends and family are telling us we should be more outspoken, quieter, smaller, larger, happier, not so happy.

Set aside everything you think you know about yourself. There is a diamond inside of you ready to shine and make an impact on this world. Let's dust it off and give you a brilliant chance to be the unique light you were made to be.

Strength-Finder Questionnaire:

(Write your answers in the space given or on a separate sheet of paper)

- What or who inspires you?

- What talents do you have?

- What things do you excel at in business, work, your home life, and hobbies? Write them all down. Brainstorm on how others have complimented you.

- What subject could you read 100 books on and not get bored?

- What would you do for five years without getting paid?

- What made you unique as a child?

- What did you love doing as a child?

- What are your top 5 things you enjoy now?

- What things have you dreamed about doing and have not had the opportunity to do yet?

- Think about the last time you were challenged. How did you overcome? Were you calm and collected, a quick thinker? Able to hide and blend in? Write down a few difficult situations you've been in, and how you solved the problem. Is there a common way you thrive through difficult situations?

- When have you felt STRONG, INVIGORATED, INQUISITIVE, SUCCESSFUL?

- What compliments do you tend to brush off? This could be things you don't think are great, but everyone around notices. Things that you do that come so natural you've always thought everyone else can do that too.

- Visualization: Imagine you just woke up excited, jumping out of bed. The sun is shining and today you are excited to ...

- What would you do with your life if you had all the money and time in the world?

- What legacy do you want to leave?

Great job! You now know more about yourself than most people do. Taking the time to sit back and be true to yourself is the first step in being the change in this world. For those of you who are convinced now more than ever that you want to take up the call to arms against human trafficking, welcome to the club. It's time to apply what you just discovered about yourself.

Think about the things you are passionate about. Think about your gifting's, talents, job skills and passion. Take time to re-read your answers above and really ponder on what makes you, YOU.

Step 4: Putting it all together

Circle the top two types of human trafficking you are the most equipped to tackle.

LABOR TRAFFICKING

FORCED MARRIAGE

ORGAN TRAFFICKING

SEX TRAFFICKING

Now ask yourself if you are more passionate about helping those in bondage in your CITY or INTERNATIONALLY?

Is there a place in your city you are drawn to?

Is there a country that has always been on your heart?

Take a moment to think about these things and journal your thoughts.

I hope you're having fun. I'm enjoying thinking about all of you and imagining big light bulbs turning on above your heads as you get clarity.

You know what they say:

"CLARITY IS POWER."

Below is an extensive list of tasks that you can do to help end human trafficking. I want you to meditate on each task and think about if it's better suited to an extrovert or introvert.

Is the task better suited for a D, I, S, or C personality?

Is it something you're passionate about?

As you read through the many different ways to fight human trafficking, highlight the task that jumps out at you and fits your strengths and personality.

- Program the hotline number into your phone

- Volunteer with the HOTLINE

- Share the hotline number with everyone you know

- Leave the hotline number at high-risk places

- Share or gift this book with as many people as you can

- Share the Top 10 ways to fight human trafficking

found in this book

- Start a Meetup or group

- Start a book club

- Join or create a local task force

- Join or create a state advisory board

- Hold an event to raise awareness

- Host a movie night at your home

- Create a community watch task force

- Create a human trafficking division of your chamber of commerce

- Educate yourself

- Learn the indicators of human trafficking

- Read books

- Watch movies

- Subscribe to blogs

- Start a blog

- Read articles

- Get trained by a local organization to teach awareness training to businesses, first responders, law enforcement, educators, federal employees, and employees in transportation

- Speak at local clubs, chambers, churches, small groups, and conferences

- Speak at school rallies

- Speak at parent's night or have a table in the hallways.
- Bring in speakers at your local club, chamber, church, small group, etc.

- Train employees at truck stops, airports, and bus stations

- Help educate inner-city teachers, non-profits, and volunteers

- Host an awareness city meeting, picnic or breakfast

- Hold an awareness seminar at your local library

- Sponsor a table at a seminar, conference or trade show

- Create and hand out gift bags with goodies and the hotline number

- Sponsor a recovered child

- Use the power of social media. Repost. share, raise awareness

- Hang up posters at truck and bus stops

- Volunteer at a local homeless shelter

- Volunteer at a center for runaway teens

- Fitness instructors: use the end of class to raise awareness

- Have a fit-a-thon benefiting survivors

- Be a foster care parent

- Research carefully before adopting as to where the child actually came from

- Ask for help with abstaining from pornography or buying sex

- Burn all your pornography

- Don't buy sex

- Advocate for a rescue center or local organization

- Be a spokesperson for an organization

- Start an annual 5K run or fundraiser supporting your favorite organization

- Participate in a local 5K run or fundraiser

- Sponsor a 5K run or fundraiser with your business or help find sponsors

- Donate your expertise, services or resources

- Lobby local policymakers

- Get involved with human trafficking legislation; sign up for alerts and be a voice

- Write your local, state and federal officials

- Talk to your local law enforcement

- Talk to your local FBI or ICE office

- Demand corporate accountability

- Avoid products and companies that facilitate human trafficking

- Download a fair-trade app

- Discover your slavery footprint

- Buy products that support survivors

Students and parents of school-age kids:

- Start a club at your school, college, or kids' school

- Write a book report, research paper, or other paper on the issue

- Encourage schools to study modern-day slavery in their curriculum

- Host a school-wide conference on the issue

- Bring in an organization to speak to your class or club

- Start a prayer group

Employees:

- Pursue a career in social work, psychology, or therapy

- Work as a first responder, FBI agent, or other law enforcement officer

- Ask your employer for a volunteer paid day off

- Create an awareness day and bring in donuts for everyone

- If you're a lawyer, you can donate your time in defending victims of human trafficking

- Social workers and psychologists can volunteer to work with victims

Business Owners:

- Use your business to sponsor fundraisers

- Give 1% of your business profits to fighting human trafficking

- Give your employees a volunteer paid day off

- Don't allow business money for purchasing sex or visiting such establishments

- Hold an awareness seminar and provide free food for the employees.

- Create jobs for survivors

Go back through them and use a pen to circle 5-8 that you are excited about and would want to do.

You're doing an excellent job! Did anything resonate with you?

I told you that I would empower you to make a difference. The start of this book is full of doom and gloom. It's hard to imagine that all over the world people are trapped in slavery; little girls and boys are being raped and sold for cash. I believe we were created for such a time as this. I believe with a conviction that every single one of you reading this book has been given a gift and a light that will be part of helping to set the captives free.

Every single one of you can program a number into your phone, remember the indicators, and tell another person to do the same thing. There is hope, and we shall shine a light into the darkness.

Slavery will no longer be able to exist in our cities, states, and great nation.

Next, think about how much time you honestly have to commit to fighting human trafficking? An hour? A day? A month? Look at your calendar and commitments. Maybe you only can commit to one weekend a year. It's something.

Write down how much time you are willing and able to commit to for the next year.

Now think about your financial commitments. How much are you able to give? Maybe it's a one-time commitment or a monthly contribution.

Write down what you will commit to for the next year.

Great! You understand who you are a little better, what talents you have to offer, where your passion is, and how much time you can commit to it. Let's put it all together and write it out. It's said that when you write something down, you are 80% more likely to accomplish it.

Writing things down encourages your brain to figure out how to make it happen. It's proven by science. Now it's time to create your action guide. Make a copy of it and hang it up on your bathroom mirror, carry it with you, or email it to yourself.

<u>NOTES</u>

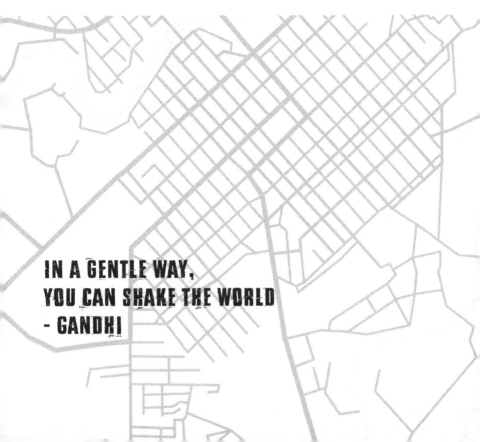

IN A GENTLE WAY,
YOU CAN SHAKE THE WORLD
- GANDHI

6   ACTION PLAN

ACTION PLAN

Fill in each section and assign a date to when you plan on accomplishing each task. Then, check them off when completed. Use your answers from Action Guide.

1- Program the hotline number into your phone:

Take out your phone right now and program this number into it:
Call: 1-888-373-7888
Text: 233733

Extra Credit: Find out if you have a local number. Call your police station and ask them questions. Find out who is in charge of human trafficking cases in your area.

2- Review the action guide and your answers about who you are and what you enjoy doing. Take a moment to meditate on your personality and the D.I.S.C test.

Think about your strengths and passions and choose the top 5 tasks you want to do.

Chances are there is a national organization that has a mission that fits with your passions. For example, if you are passionate about labor trafficking and have a law background, International Justice Mission would be an excellent organization for you to get involved with.

Write down the top 5 tasks you would like to implement.

1)

2)

3)

4)

5)

3- Now, you need to decide where you want to make an impact. Locally, internationally, or both. Write down the state, city or community you want to impact locally. Then write what country you want to impact internationally.

Local:

International:

4- Next, it's time to find an organization that is aligned with your passion, strengths, and geographic location. This may take some time and research. Start with searching on the internet for the words "fight human trafficking" and the task you most want to do.

Write down up to 3 organizations you would want to get involved with.

1)

2)

3)

Circle your favorite organization out of the top three—maybe one local and one international.

Here are some I recommend as of the publishing of this book:

Operation Underground Railroad- ourrescue.org
Love 146- love146.org
She Rescue Home- sherescuehome.org
National Human Trafficking Survivor Coalition- nhtsc.com

5- Find the answers to these questions. You can use websites like, Guidestar or Great Non-profits to research if the organizations are doing what they say they are.

Organization Name:

When did they start up?

What is their story?

How much of their donations go to helping survivors?

Do they have a local chapter you can join?

What is their national contact info and local contact info?

National:

Local:

Here are some tips for when you contact them:

Ask questions about what volunteer opportunities they have that line up with your strengths and passion.

Contact your local chapter and attend a meeting to see if you like the people who are going. You will be spending lots of time with them. See if they are open to your ideas of how you can help. If the first organization is not responsive, or the volunteers are not your peeps, go through your list until you find the right fit for you.

All you have to do now is plug in and enjoy being part of the solution.

Maybe you realized you only have time for one event this year. Is it hosting a movie at your house? Is it running in a 5k while raising donations?

6-Write out what you will do and when you will accomplish it.

Put it on your calendar and plan to commit.
Example: I will: Call my local chapter of Love146. Offer to help with their yearly fundraiser by June 2019.

I will:

By (month)_____ (year)_____

It's just that easy to get involved in the battle against human trafficking. You may never see the effect of your actions, but remember the butterfly effect? A small butterfly would never understand that by doing what it is naturally made to do, it can produce a significant impact on the world around them.

Just be you. Do what you can.

A small impact by millions of people will create a revolution. But beware of overcommitting. Don't plan on doing all the task that you chose at one time. Do one thing at a time and when that is over or on autopilot, choose another. Our burning passion may encourage us to go and do it all at once and make huge waves. If we do that, we may drown ourselves and others around us. Focus on one task, one event, one impact at a time.

Unfortunately, human trafficking is not going anywhere any time soon. We must prepare ourselves for the long battle. We must be honest with ourselves about what we can do and then pace ourselves. The more of us that join the fight, the easier it will be to make an impact. Just go spread the word, share this book and do one small thing this week to be the change.

<u>NOTES</u>

<u>NOTES</u>

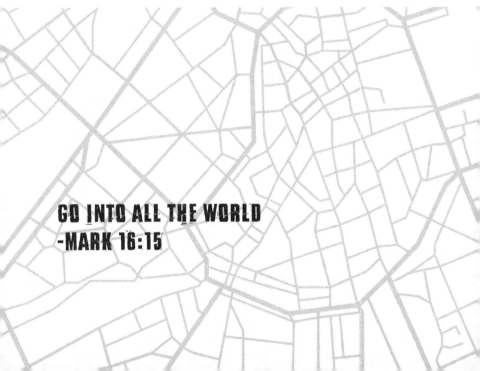

GO INTO ALL THE WORLD
-MARK 16:15

GO

GO

I am so impressed that you have stuck with me through this whole book! I know when you first picked it up you may not have been prepared for everything you discovered. I have been told that most people only read the first three chapters of a book, so if you finished this book, you are not like most people. I didn't expect you to be. I envisioned my readers being extraordinary, ordinary people, living what looks like a normal life on the outside, but on the inside of them is the most amazing gifts, strengths, and talents just waiting to be used for good in this world. Thank you for caring.

You could have chosen one of those trendy life empowerment books. You know, the books that are filled with "ra-ra" and help you become the next big mogul. Instead, you choose to care, and read this book. Not only read it but apply it and commit to making a difference.

If I were there with you, I would give you a gold star and a big hug. I may even tear up as I'm hugging you. Great, even the end of this book is making me cry.

For too long I thought the little things I was doing to make an impact didn't matter. I would feel insignificant when hearing about how someone started a non-profit and is now rescuing babies in another country, or how so and so did such and such. We've all felt inadequate before.

But not anymore. I no longer feel that way, and never want you to feel like that either.

When I got the revelation that we all can create a butterfly effect, my perspective changed. I knew I must create a message that would inspire everyone to do one small, kind act. I wanted you to know how talented you are, no matter what your background, ethnicity, or financial situation. We all have little gifts inside of us to share and shine into this world. We are all uniquely and wonderfully made. We were all created for such a time as this.

So, GO! Go into your neighborhood, city, nation and the world.

Go shine your light and be who you were created to be. Use your gifts, strengths, and passion to make a difference for good in this world. It's never too late.

If after reading this, you realize that you have been part of the problem, it's okay. Take action and start making the changes towards being part of the solution. Have a big bonfire and burn up all your porn and vow to treat women with respect. Go find a place to get help and counseling.

Start buying fair-trade chocolate bars and socially responsible cotton tee-shirts. Research where your diamonds came from. Be a socially responsible and shop ethically.

You are now equipped and empowered to go and answer the battle cry against human trafficking. You have created an action plan for taking small steps towards victory. You have the information you need to start a revolution of change.

GO!! And don't forget to send me your stories about how you are making a difference. You can find me on all social media @amandamayfoltz and use the hashtags #battlecryHT and #bashslavery to share on social media.

Visit my website at amandafoltz.com to follow me and see what trouble I'm causing next.

I love you all! You are all amazing warriors, and I'm honored to be a small part of your journey.

NOTES

COURAGE, DEAR HEART
-C.S. LEWIS

THE LIST

THE LIST

- Program the hotline number into your phone

- Volunteer with the HOTLINE

- Share the hotline number with everyone you know

- Leave the hotline number at high-risk places

- Share or gift this book with as many people as you can

- Share the Top 10 ways to fight human trafficking found in this book

- Start a Meetup or group

- Start a book club

- Join or create a local task force

- Join or create a state advisory board

- Hold an event to raise awareness

- Host a movie night at your home

- Create a community watch task force

- Create a human trafficking division of your chamber of commerce

- Educate yourself

- Learn the indicators of human trafficking

- Read books

- Watch movies

- Subscribe to blogs

- Start a blog

- Read articles

- Get trained by a local organization to teach awareness training to businesses, first responders, law enforcement, educators, federal employees, and employees in transportation

- Speak at local clubs, chambers, churches, small groups, and conferences

- Speak at school rallies

- Speak at parent's night or have a table in the hallways.
- Bring in speakers at your local club, chamber, church, small group, etc.

- Train employees at truck stops, airports, and bus stations

- Help educate inner-city teachers, non-profits, and volunteers

- Host an awareness city meeting, picnic or breakfast

- Hold an awareness seminar at your local library

- Sponsor a table at a seminar, conference or trade show

- Create and hand out gift bags with goodies and the hotline number

- Sponsor a recovered child

- Use the power of social media. Repost. share, raise awareness

- Hang up posters at truck and bus stops

- Volunteer at a local homeless shelter

- Volunteer at a center for runaway teens

- Fitness instructors: use the end of class to raise awareness

- Have a fit-a-thon benefiting survivors

- Be a foster care parent

- Research carefully before adopting as to where the child actually came from

- Ask for help with abstaining from pornography or buying sex

- Burn all your pornography

- Don't buy sex

- Advocate for a rescue center or local organization

- Be a spokesperson for an organization

- Start an annual 5K run or fundraiser supporting your favorite organization

- Participate in a local 5K run or fundraiser

- Sponsor a 5K run or fundraiser with your business or help find sponsors

- Donate your expertise, services or resources

- Lobby local policymakers

- Get involved with human trafficking legislation; sign up for alerts and be a voice

- Write your local, state and federal officials

- Talk to your local law enforcement

- Talk to your local FBI or ICE office

- Demand corporate accountability

- Avoid products and companies that facilitate human trafficking

- Download a fair-trade app

- Discover your slavery footprint

- Buy products that support survivors

Students and parents of school-age kids:

- Start a club at your school, college, or kids' school

- Write a book report, research paper, or other paper on the issue

- Encourage schools to study modern-day slavery in their curriculum

- Host a school-wide conference on the issue

- Bring in an organization to speak to your class or club

- Start a prayer group

Employees:
- Pursue a career in social work, psychology, or therapy

- Work as a first responder, FBI agent, or other law enforcement officer

- Ask your employer for a volunteer paid day off

- Create an awareness day and bring in donuts for

everyone

- If you're a lawyer, you can donate your time in defending victims of human trafficking

- Social workers and psychologists can volunteer to work with victims

Business Owners:

- Use your business to sponsor fundraisers

- Give 1% of your business profits to fighting human trafficking

- Give your employees a volunteer paid day off

- Don't allow business money for purchasing sex or visiting such establishments

- Hold an awareness seminar and provide free food for the employees.

- Create jobs for survivors

THE SMALLEST ACT OF KINDNESS IS WORTH
MORE THAN THE GRANDEST INTENTION
-OSCAR WILDE

TOP 10

TOP 10
WAYS TO FIGHT HUMAN TRAFFICKING

#1 Save the hotline number in your phone

If there is only one thing you do, let it be this! Save the hotline number in your phone and share it with as many people possible.
Call: 1-888-373-7888
Text: 233733
If you see anything call the number and report it.

#2 Learn the indicators of human trafficking
Be an aware citizen and learn the indicators of human trafficking. There are signs that you can look for to identify possible trafficking situations.
- Physical abuse
- Seem fearful
- Not allowed to talk for themselves
- No passport or docs
- Not free to leave
- Lacks their own money
- Lies about age
- Branding or odd tattoo
- Dressed inappropriately
- Seems scripted

#3 Educate yourself
Knowledge is Power!
Start to devour as much information as possible on human trafficking. Read- Watch movies- Research online. Become an expert.

#4 Host a bash slavery night
Now that you have all this knowledge and awareness it's time
to share it! Host a party- (Bash Slavery party). Have friends
over to watch a movie, review a book or listen to a guest
speaker. Already having a party? Have them stay late or come
early to heart of human trafficking.

#5 Get involved
Find a goal organization that is making an impact and get
involved. Or start a blog, podcast, to highlight your favorite
abolitionists. Or GO Intl. + Join an impact trip.

#6 Shop wisely
Be an aware consumer. Look for labels that say they have fair
practices. Buy items made from survivors as gifts.

#7 Lobby local politicians
Write your local politicians and explain to them the severity of
human trafficking. Contact your Mayor+ Chamber then voice
your opinions.

#8 Don't buy sex
Without a demand there would be no need for supply.

#9 Pray and practice gratitude
Pray for those trapped in slavery.
Practice gratitude daily

#10 Give

ABOUT THE AUTHOR

Amanda Foltz has a passion for entrepreneurship. She believes it is a gateway to freedom. She has founded multiple companies and uses them to make a difference in this world. Currently, she is Founder and CEO of Foltz International. She believes in a concept of BAM – Business as a Mission. She helps train and guide women all over the world in creating micro-enterprises to help empower them and give them dignity.

She is relentless when it comes to seeing those in bondage set free. For over a decade she has been speaking, educating and empowering others to walk in freedom. Her personal story of freedom is a testimony to the power of God's redemptive love. Her passion to end human trafficking has taken her all around the world.

Amanda and her husband, Joshua were married in 2000. They have three amazing son's. Her family graciously supports her passion to travel the world so she can spread hope and empowerment.

Amanda Foltz in India

BIBLIOGRAPHY

1. "Also of Interest." *NCCP | Child Poverty*, 26 Oct. 2012, www.nccp.org/ publications/pub_1073.html.

2. "Alternativproject" - www.alternativproject.org, 2019

3. Ballard, Tim, director. *OUR Stories*. *OUR Stories*, 13 Mar. 2018, ourrescue.org/blog/the-abolitionists-making-the-movie/.

4. Batstone, David. "Homepage." *Not For Sale*, 2007, www.notforsalecampaign.org/.

5. Collins, Amy Fine, and Larry Fink. "Sex Trafficking of Americans: The Girls Next Door." *The Hive*, Vanity Fair, 31 Jan. 2015, www.vanityfair.com/news/2011/05/sex-trafficking-201105.

6. Corbett, Steve, et al. *When Helping Hurts How to Alleviate Poverty Without Hurting the Poor ... and Yourself.* Moody Publishers, 2014.

7. Dillion, Justin, director. *Call + Response* . *Vimeo*, 1 Oct. 2008, vimeo.com/ 148655788.

8. Foundation, Walk Free. "40 Million in Modern Slavery and 152 Million in Child Labour around the World." *World Day for Safety and Health at Work 2013: Case Study: Karoshi: Death from Overwork*, 19 Sept. 2017, www.ilo.org/global/about-the-ilo/newsroom/news/ WCMS_574717/lang--en/index.htm.

9. Girls Not Brides. "About Child Marriage." *Girls Not Brides*, 2018, www.girlsnotbrides.org/about-child-marriage/.

10. "Home." *Children's Bureau | ACF*, www.acf.hhs.gov/.

11. "Hope for Justice." *Our Plan | Hope for Justice*, 2018, hopeforjustice.org/ spot-the-signs/#general-indicators https:// www.psychologytoday.com/us/blog/why-bad-looks-good/201801/ look-closer-how-spot-human-trafficking-victims https://

www.purchased.org/know-the-signs https://mashable.com/ 2016/01/12/how-to-spot-human-trafficking/#MyIbuTCNMPqh.

12. "How Many People Are On Porn Sites Right Now? (Hint: It's A Lot.)." *Fight the New Drug*, Fight the New Drug, 2 Apr. 2018, fightthenewdrug.org/by-the-numbers-see-how-many-people-are-watching-porn-today/.

13. "Human Trafficking by the Numbers." *Human Rights First*, 2017, www.humanrightsfirst.org/resource/human-trafficking-numbers.

14. "ILO." *World Day for Safety and Health at Work 2013: Case Study: Karoshi: Death from Overwork*, Walk Free Foundation and International Organization for Migration , 2017, www.ilo.org/global/topics/forced-labour/lang--en/index.htm.

15. International , Good Weave. "Better Brick Nepal." *Global Fairness Initiative*, 2015, www.globalfairness.org/our-work/our-programs/better-brick-nepal.

16. "IOMX Campaign Resources." *IOM X*, iomx.org/.

17. Jones, Kristin. "The Shepherd." *Colorado Trust*, 2 Jan. 2019, www.coloradotrust.org/content/story/shepherd.

18. Malarek, Victor. *The Natashas: the New Global Sex Trade*. Vision, 2004.

19. MCLAUGHLIN, Liam. "United Nations Office on Drugs and Crime." *Integrity in the Criminal Justice System*, 26 July 2018, www.unodc.org/unodc/en/human-trafficking/what-is-human-trafficking.html.

20. Mortenson, Greg, and David Oliver. Relin. Three Cups of Tea: One Man's Extraordinary Journey to Promote Peace -- One School at a Time. W F Howes, 2010.

21. "National Human Trafficking Survivor Coalition"- Kelly Dore - *www.nhtsc.com*

173

22. "National Sexual Violence Resource Center (NSVRC)." *Sexual Assault Statistics | National Sexual Violence Resource Center (NSVRC)*, www.nsvrc.org/.

23. Perez, Ricardo. "Sheep Header Campaign in Colorado ." *Hispanic Affairs Project* , 2013, hapgj.org.

24. "Polaris-Freedom happens now"-*https://humantraffickinghotline.org/*

25. Showalter, Misty. *"Unraveling the Web of Spain's Sweatshops."* CNN, Cable News Network, 5 July 2011, thecnnfreedomproject.blogs.cnn.com/ 2011/07/05/undercovers-crack-slave-labor-gang/.

26. Swarens, Tim. "Who Buys a Trafficked Child for Sex? Otherwise Ordinary Men." *Who Buys a Trafficked Child for Sex? Otherwise Ordinary Men*, 2018, www.usatoday.com/story/opinion/nation-now/2018/01/30/sex-trafficking-column/1073459001/.

27. "The 1 in 6 Statistic - Sexual Abuse and Assault of Boys and Men." *1in6*, 1in6.org/get-information/the-1-in-6-statistic/.

28. "The Average Age of Entry Myth." *Polaris*, 26 Oct. 2017, polarisproject.org/blog/2016/01/05/average-age-entry-myth.

29. "Trafficking in Persons Report ." *Trafficking In Persons Report* , 2018, www.state.gov/documents/organization/282798.pdf.

30. Yun, Jenny. "GEMS against Commercial Sexual Exploitation & Domestic Trafficking in the US." *Women's World Wide Web*, 9 June 2016, www.w4.org/en/wowwire/gems-sexual-exploitation-domestic-trafficking-of-girls-us/.

Made in the USA
Coppell, TX
02 August 2020